FIFTY SHADES OF MANDALA MIDNIGHT-EDITION COLORING BOOK

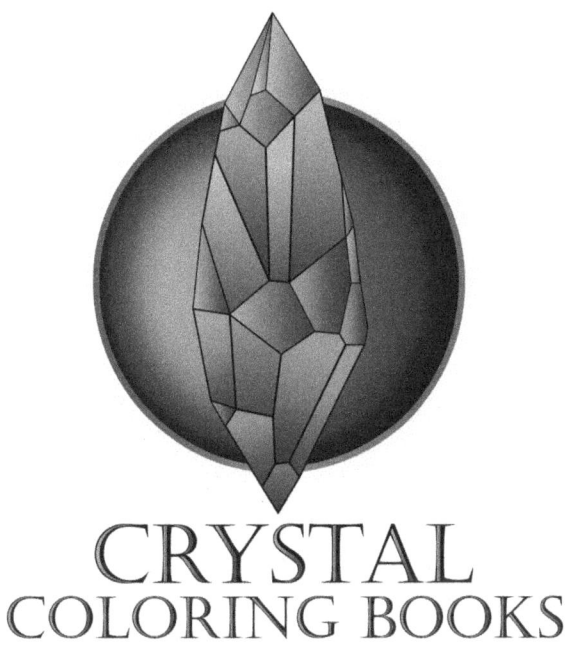

CRYSTAL
COLORING BOOKS

Copyright © 2019 Crystal Coloring Books
All rights reserved.

ISBN: 9781687312709

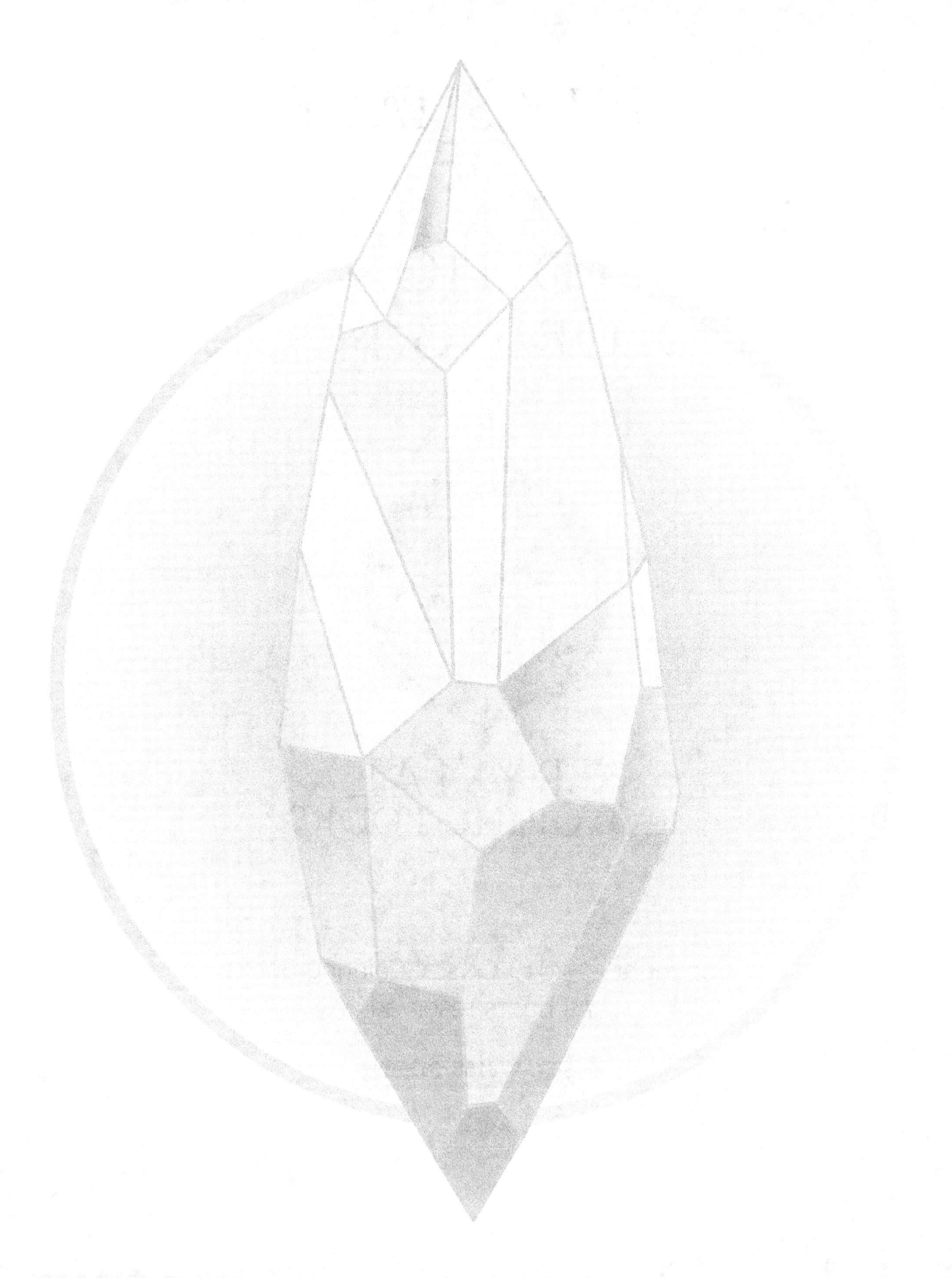

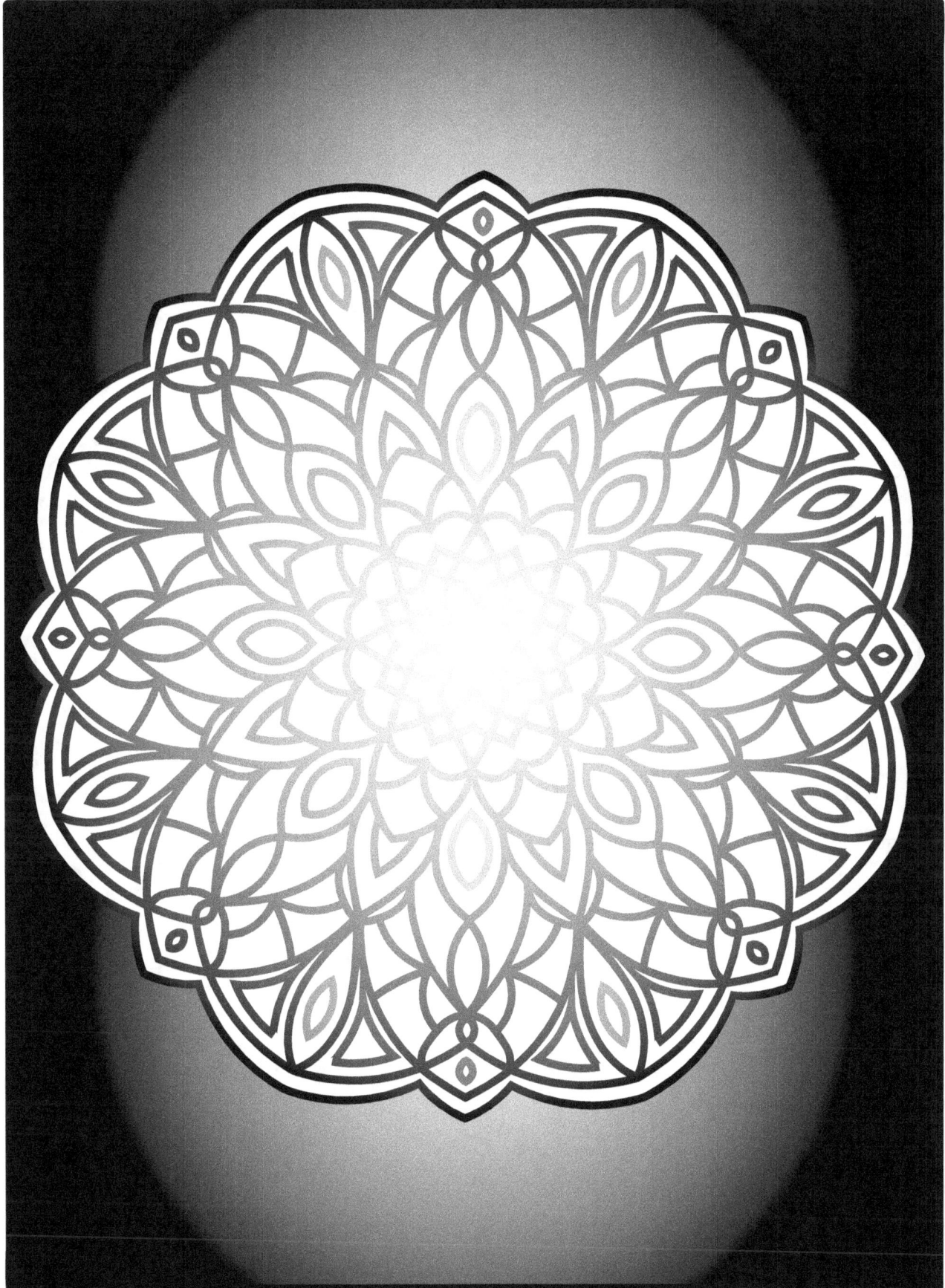

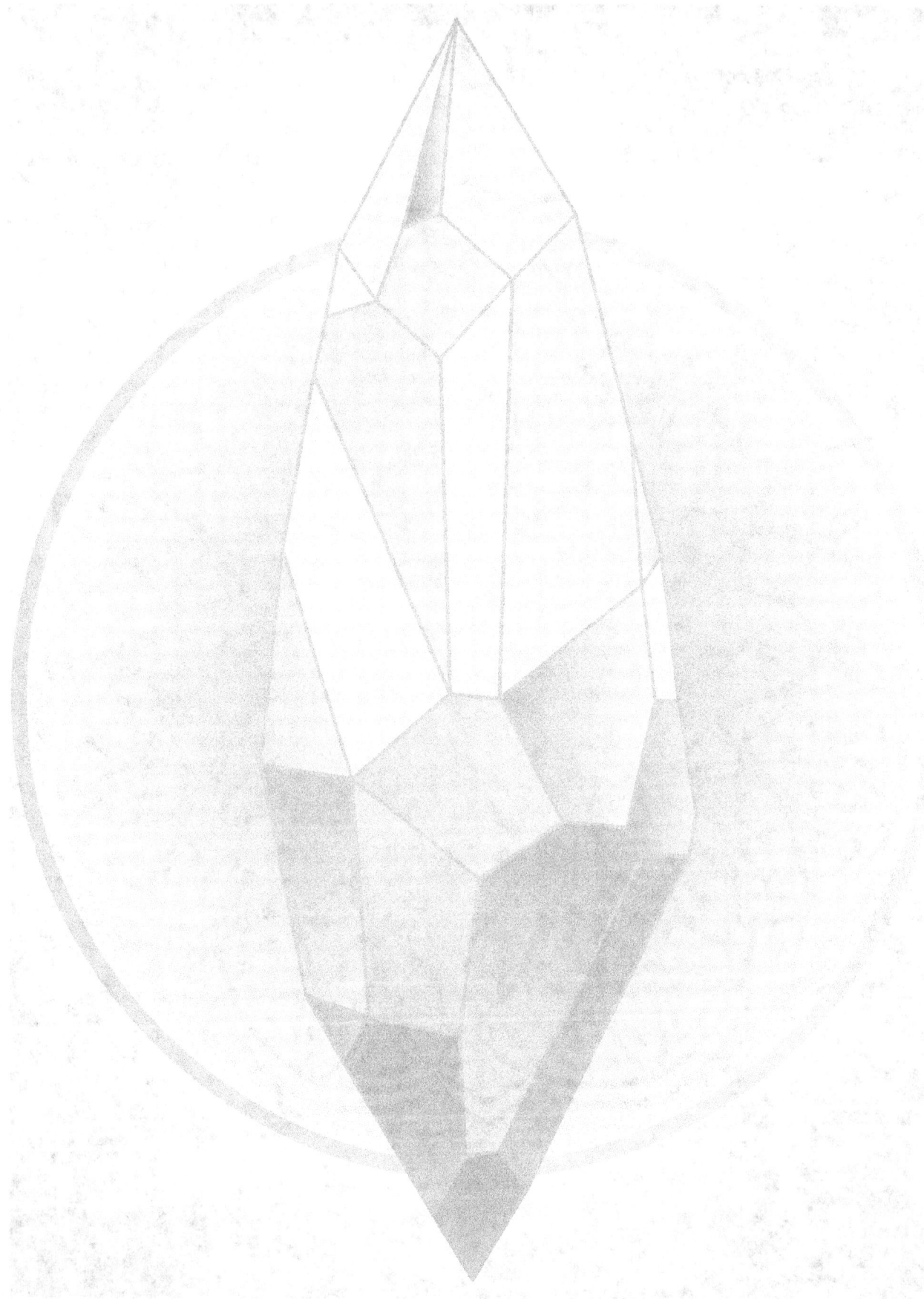

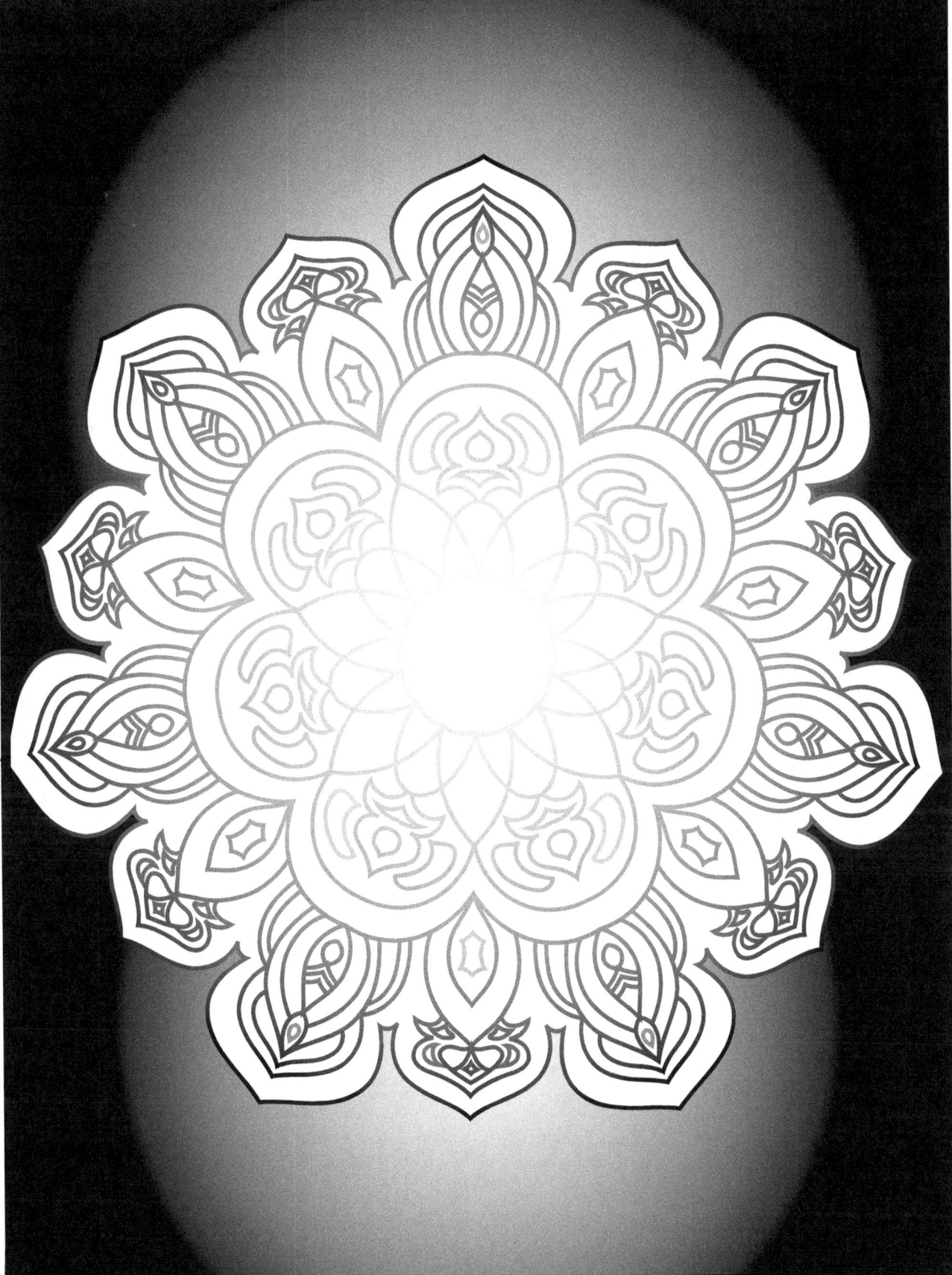

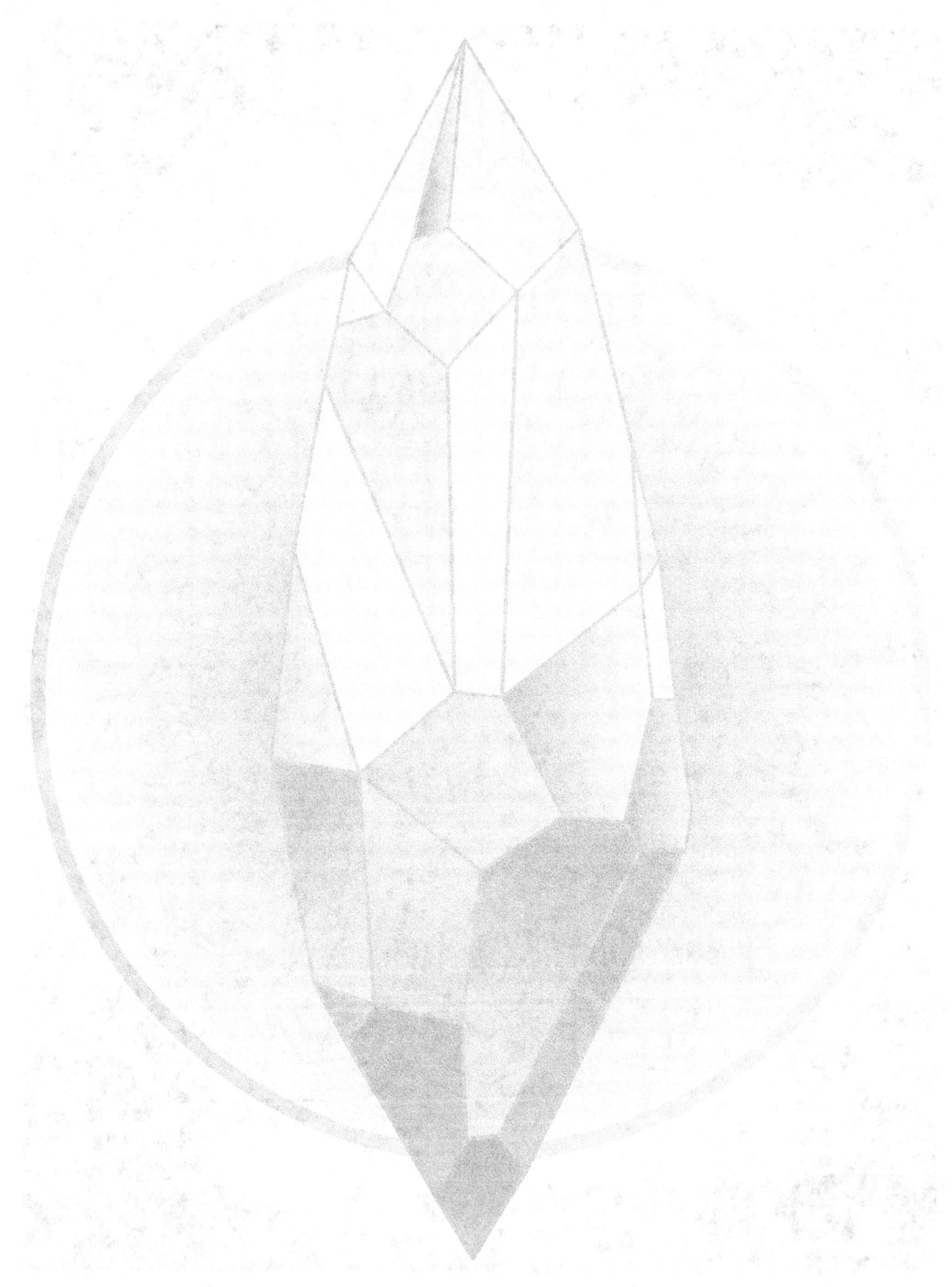

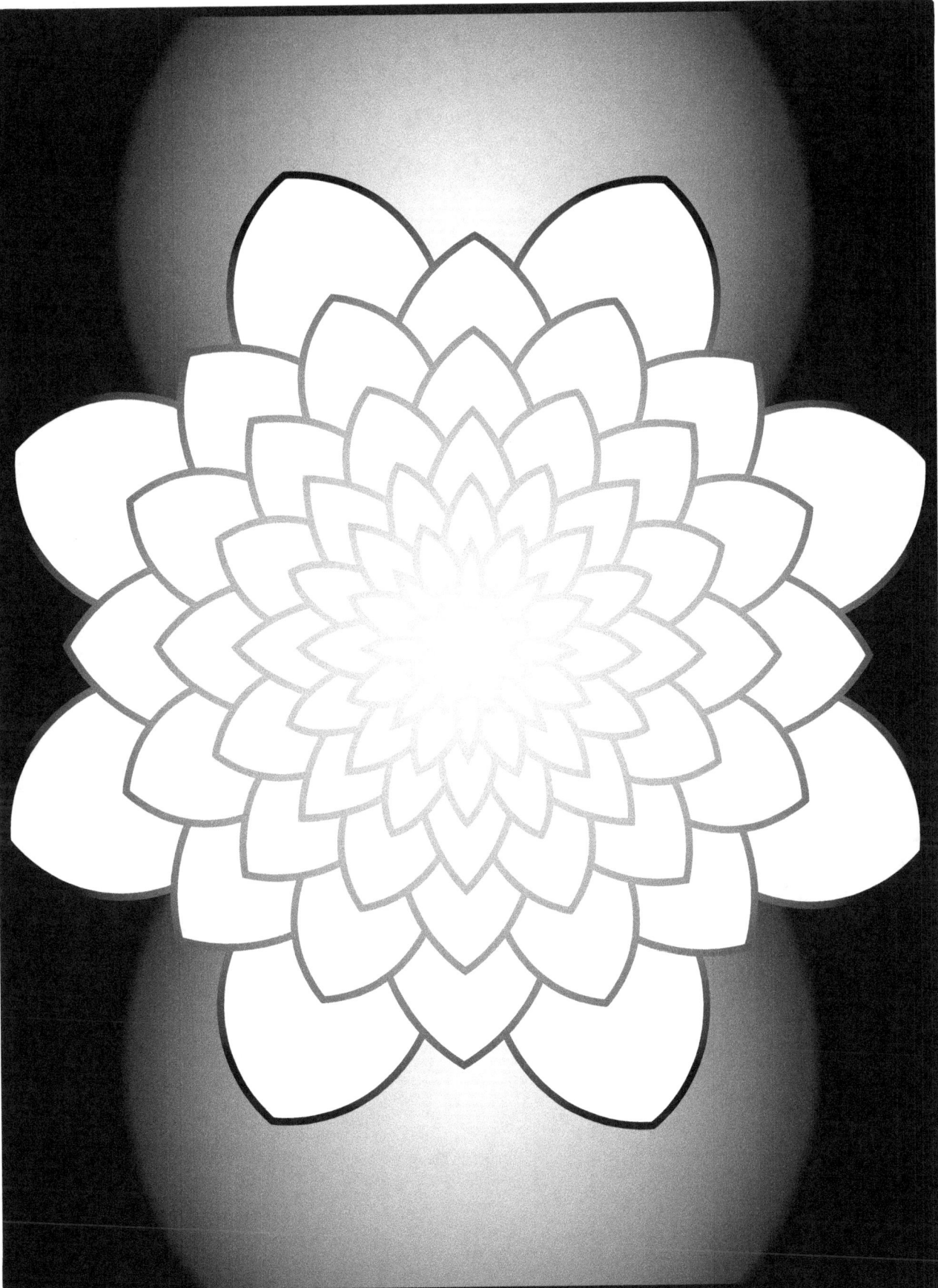

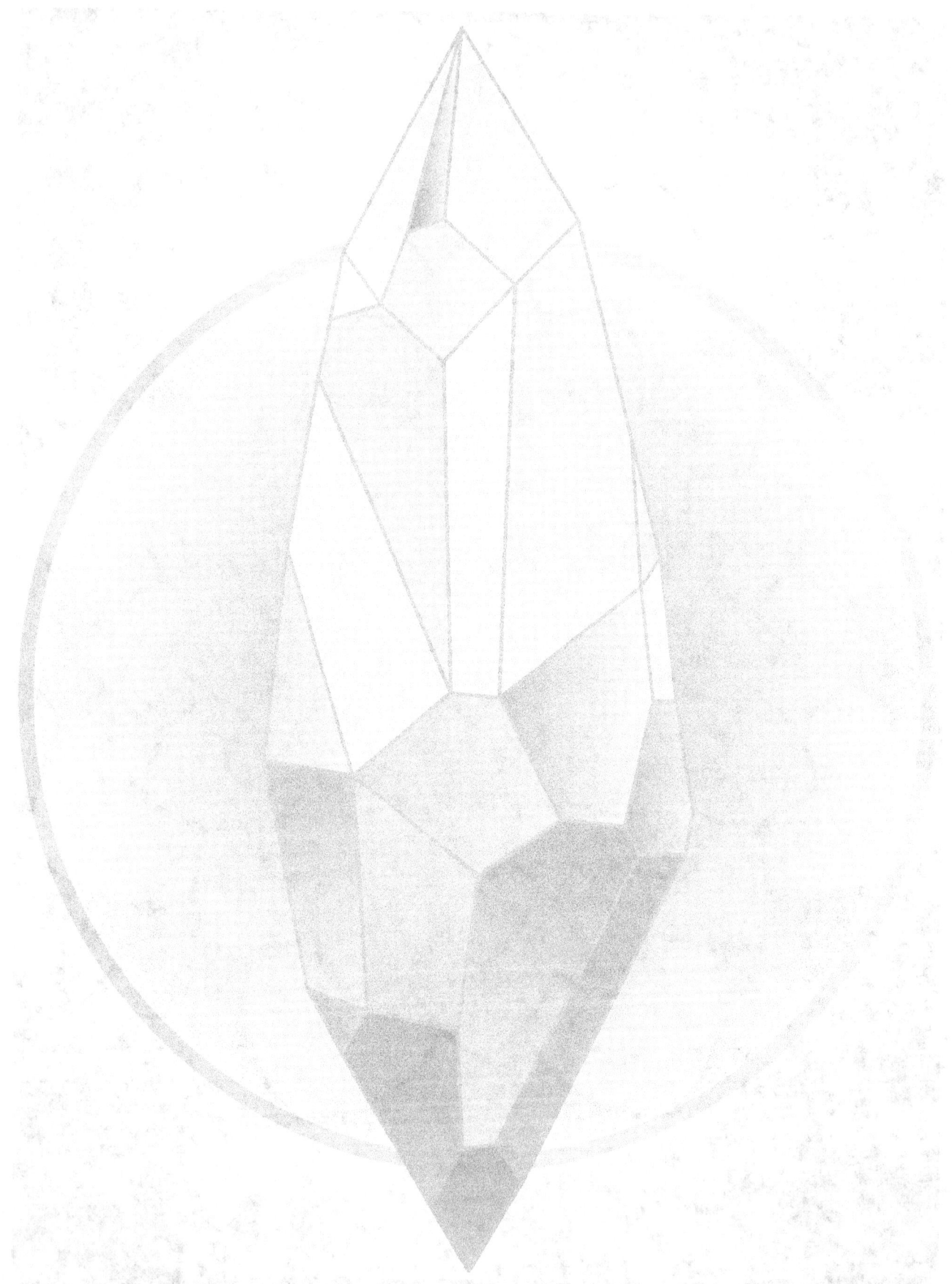

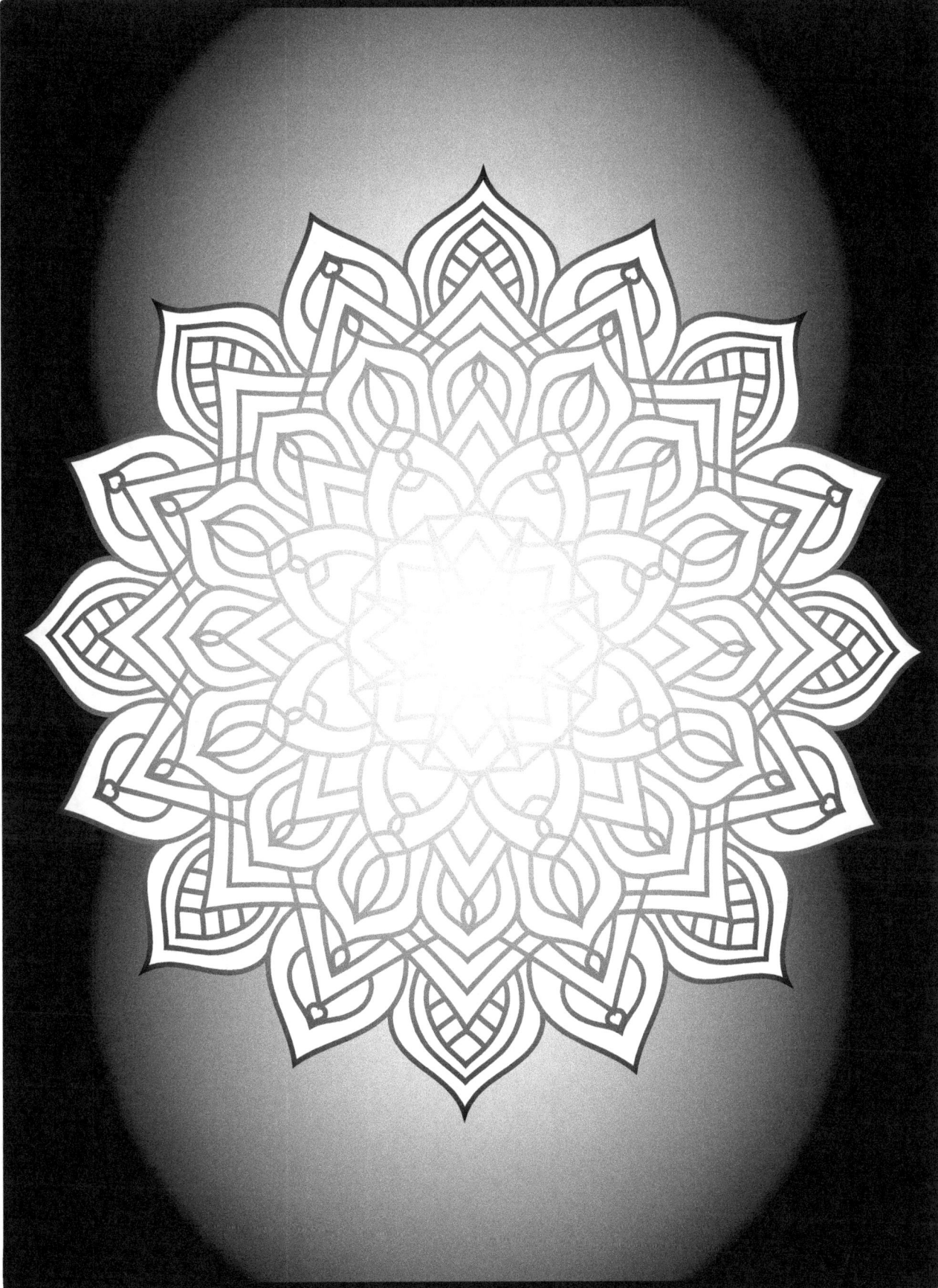

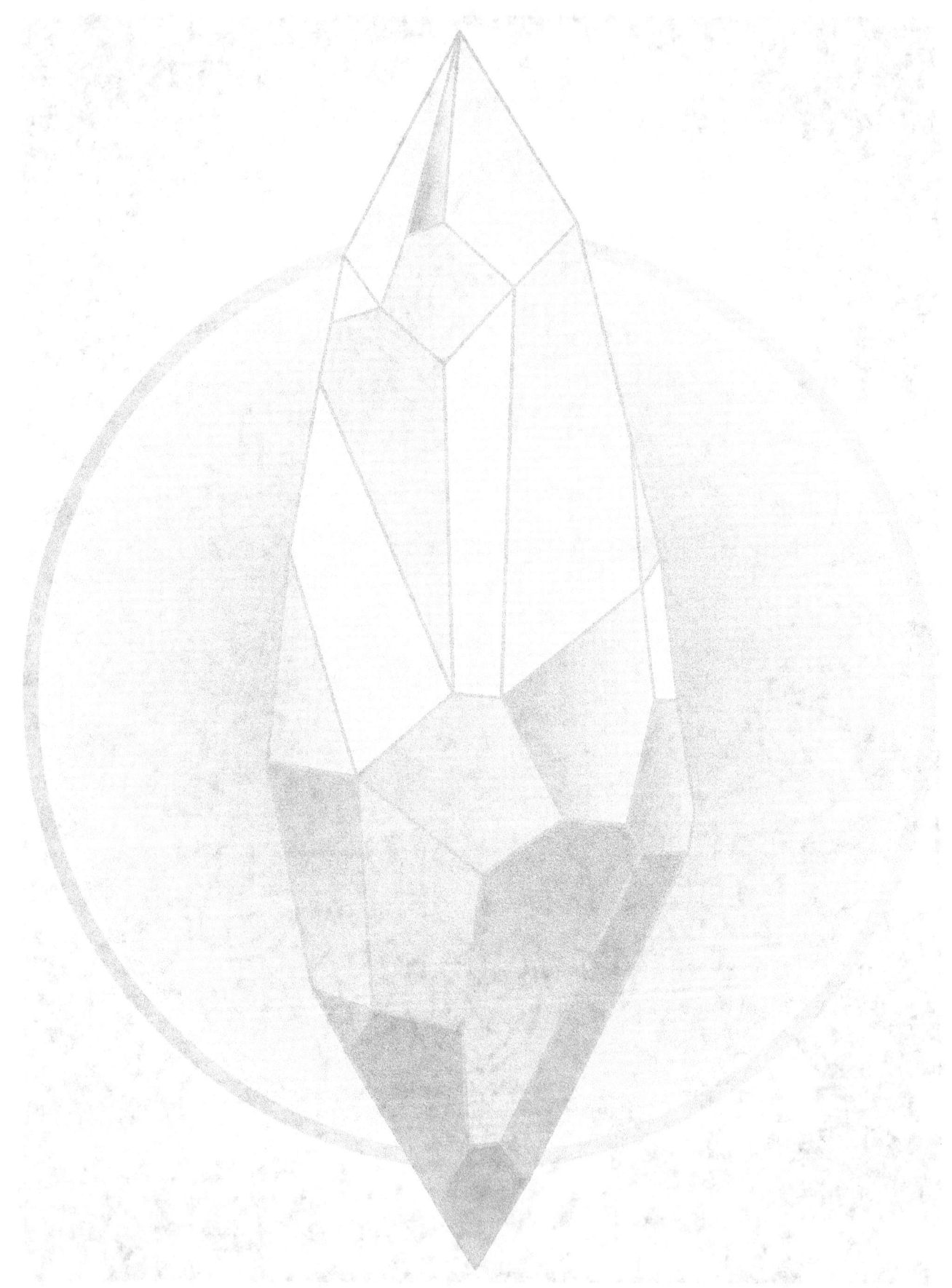

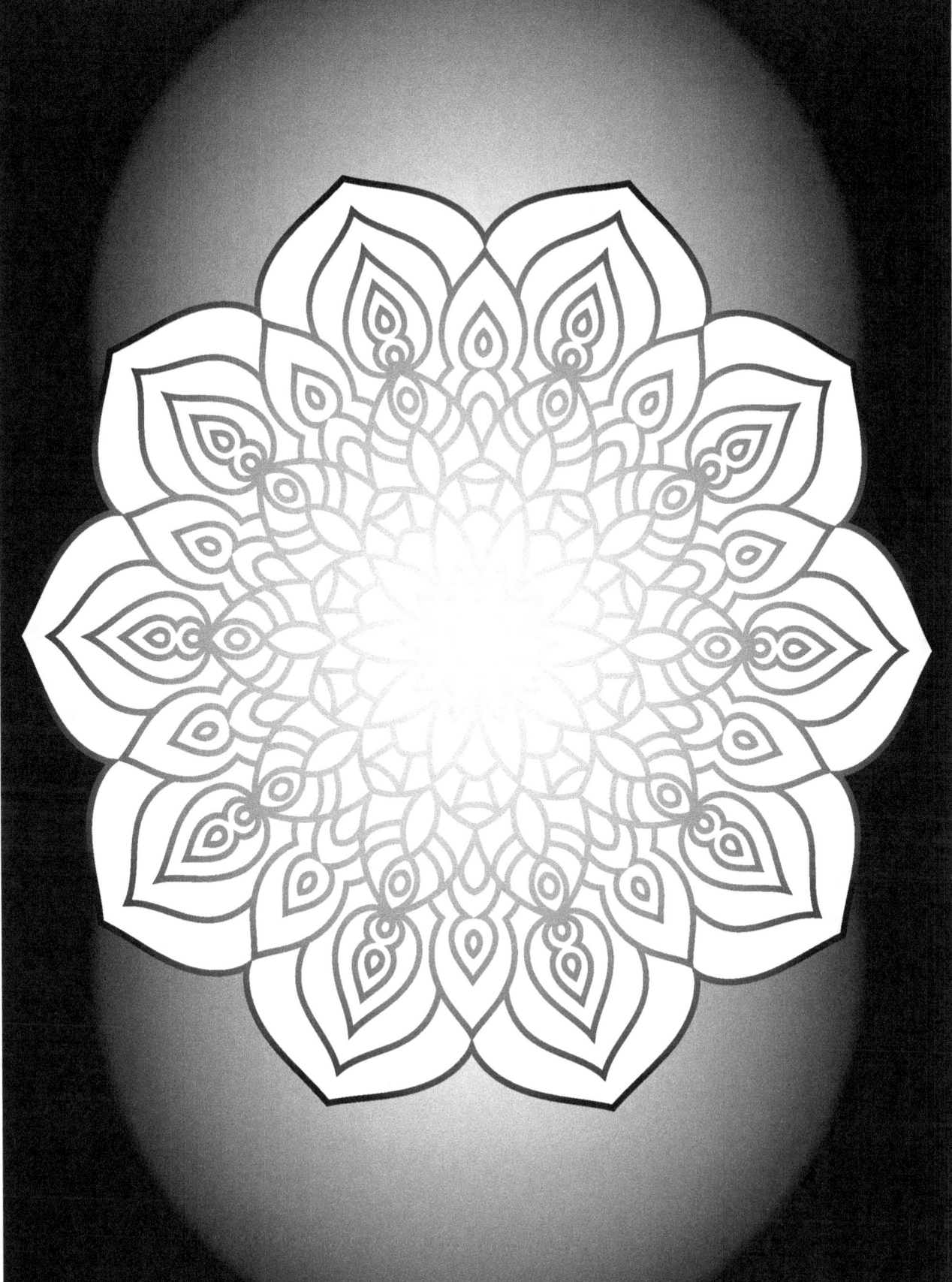

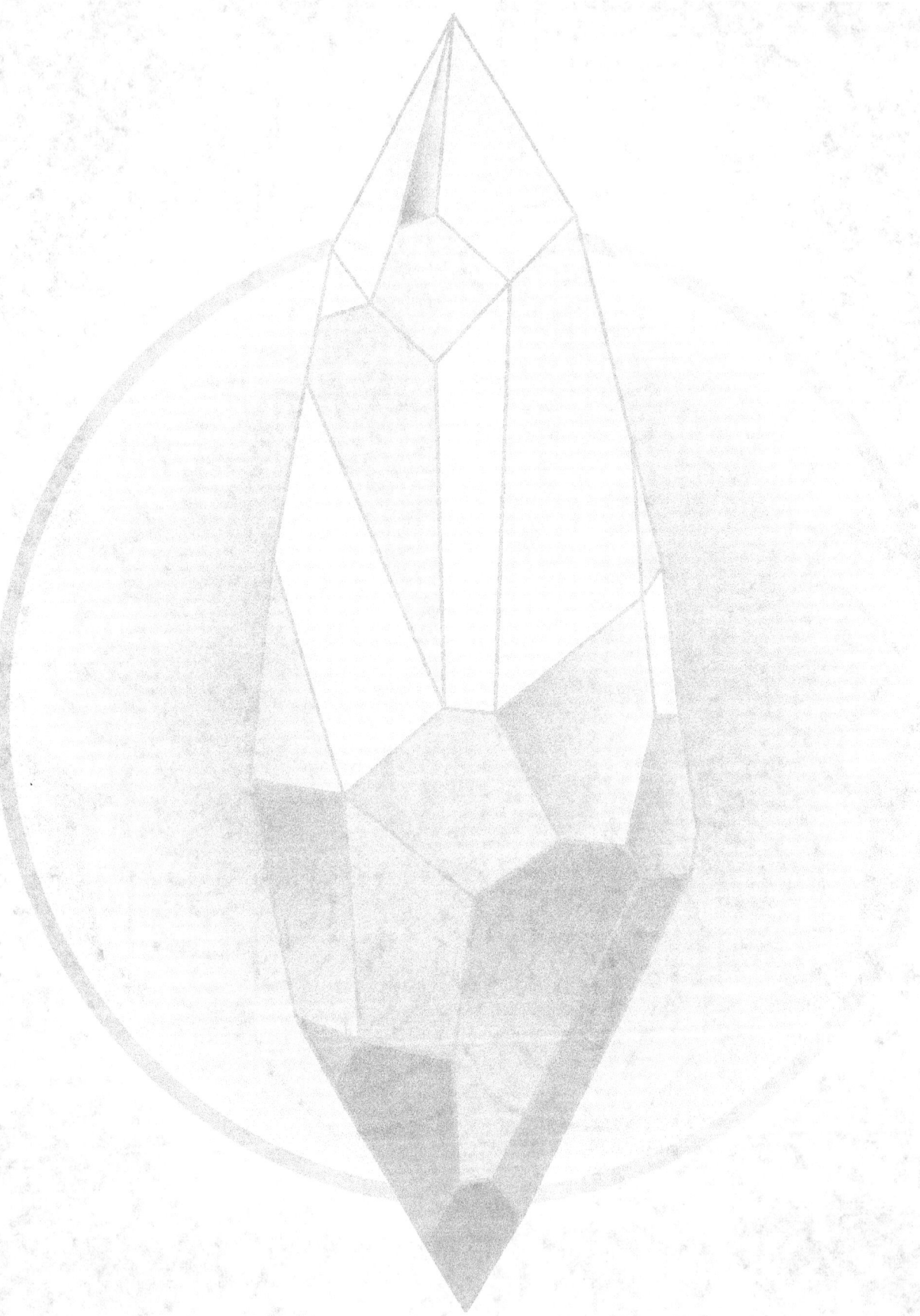

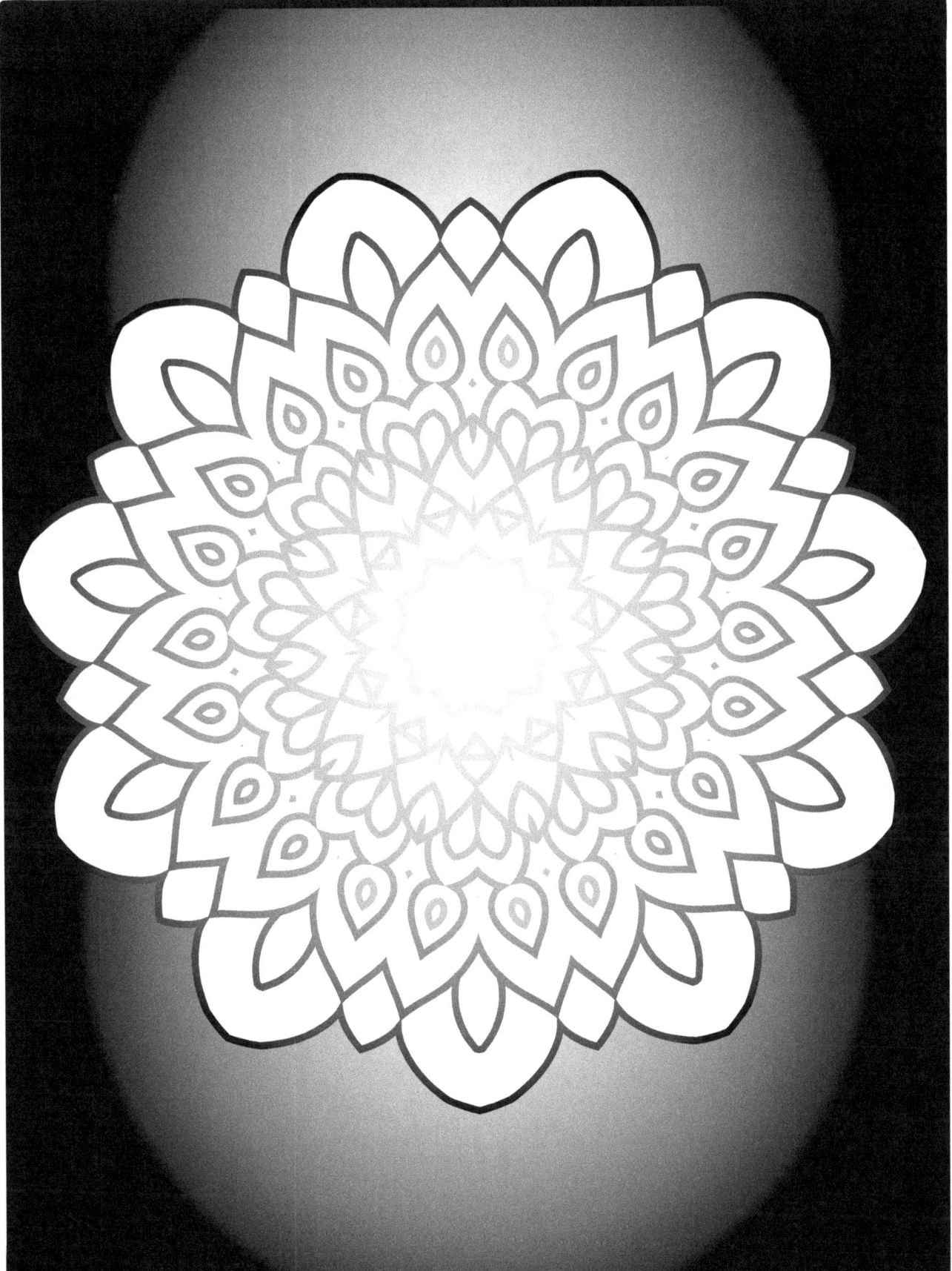

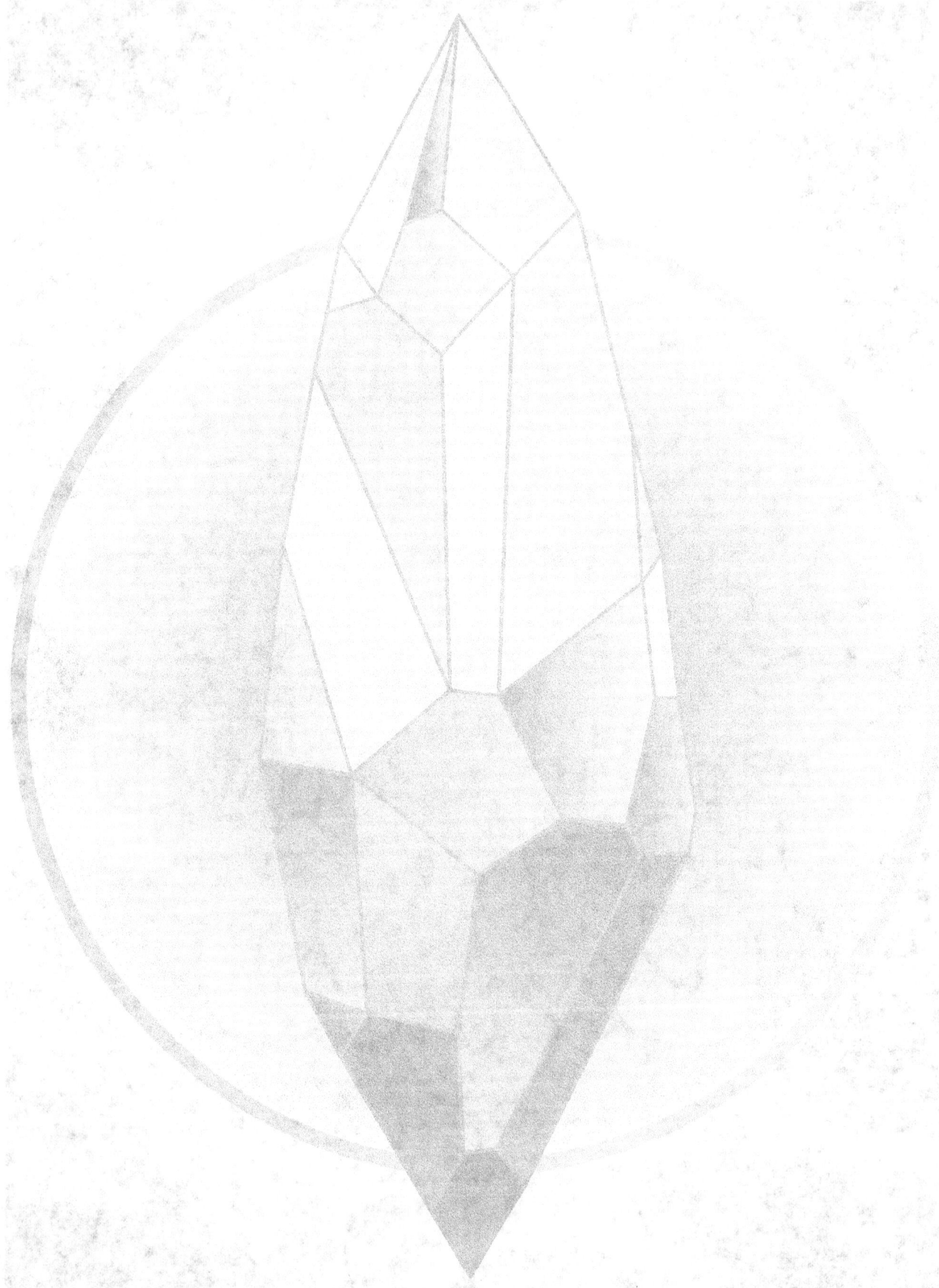

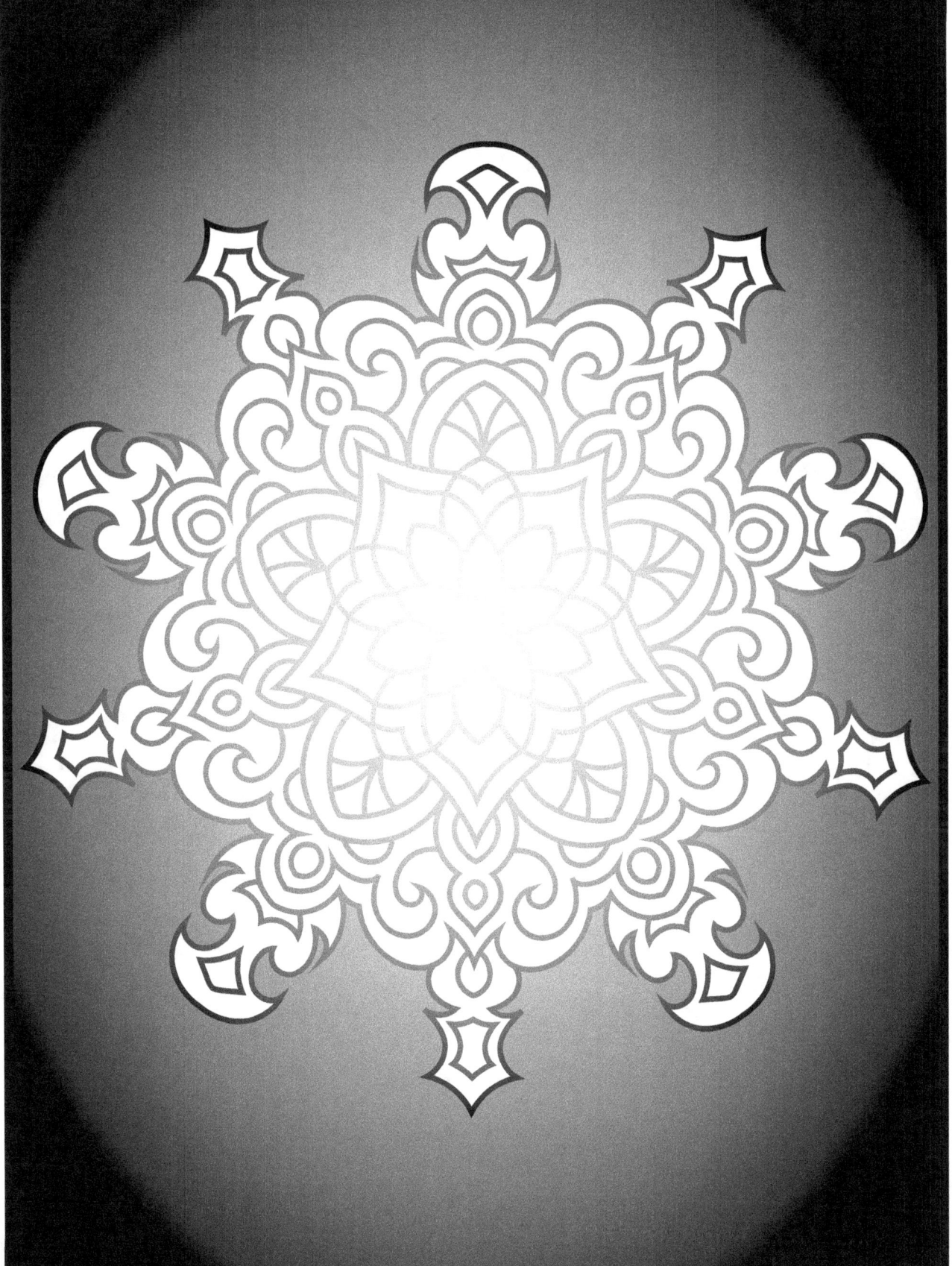

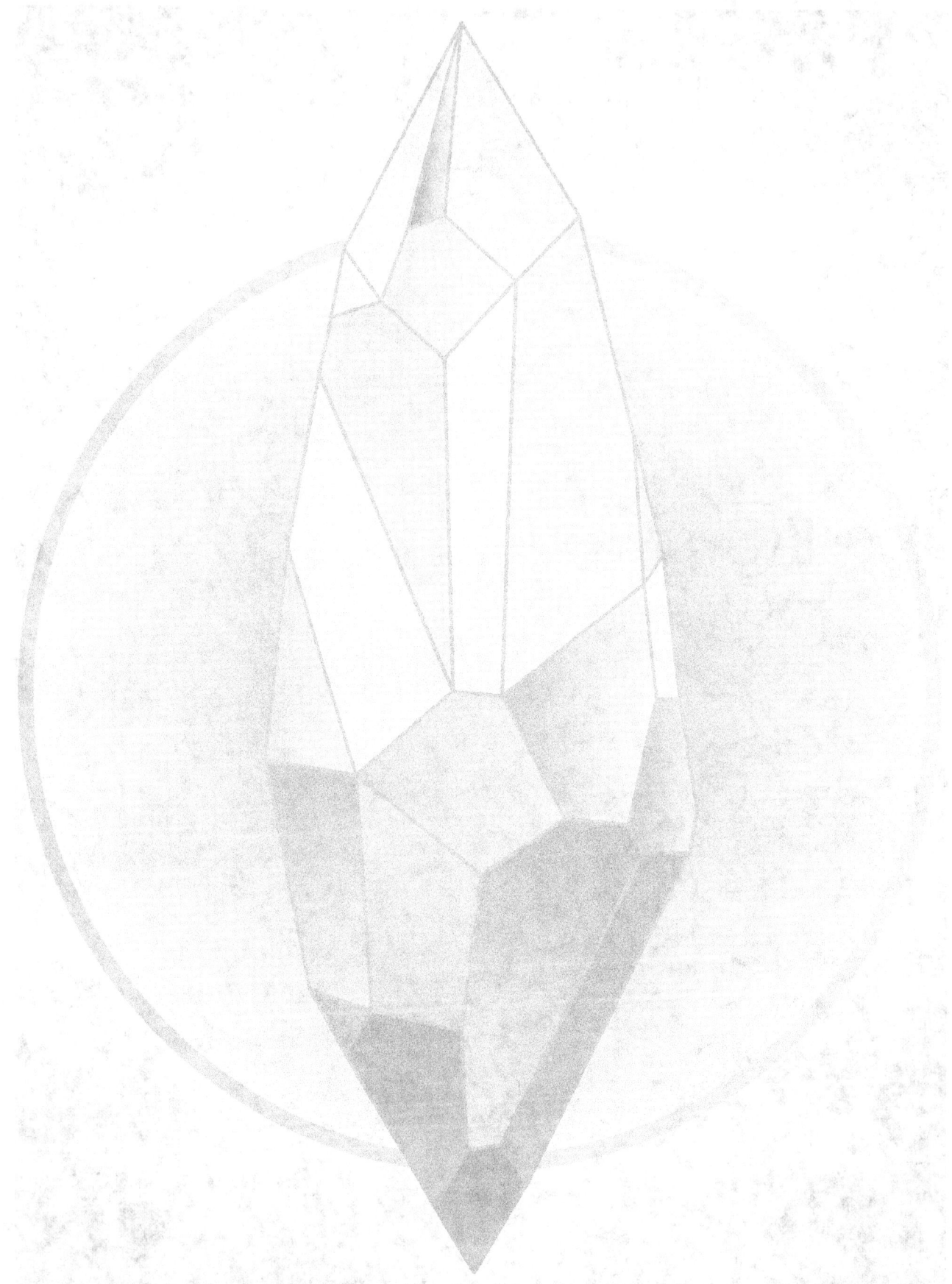

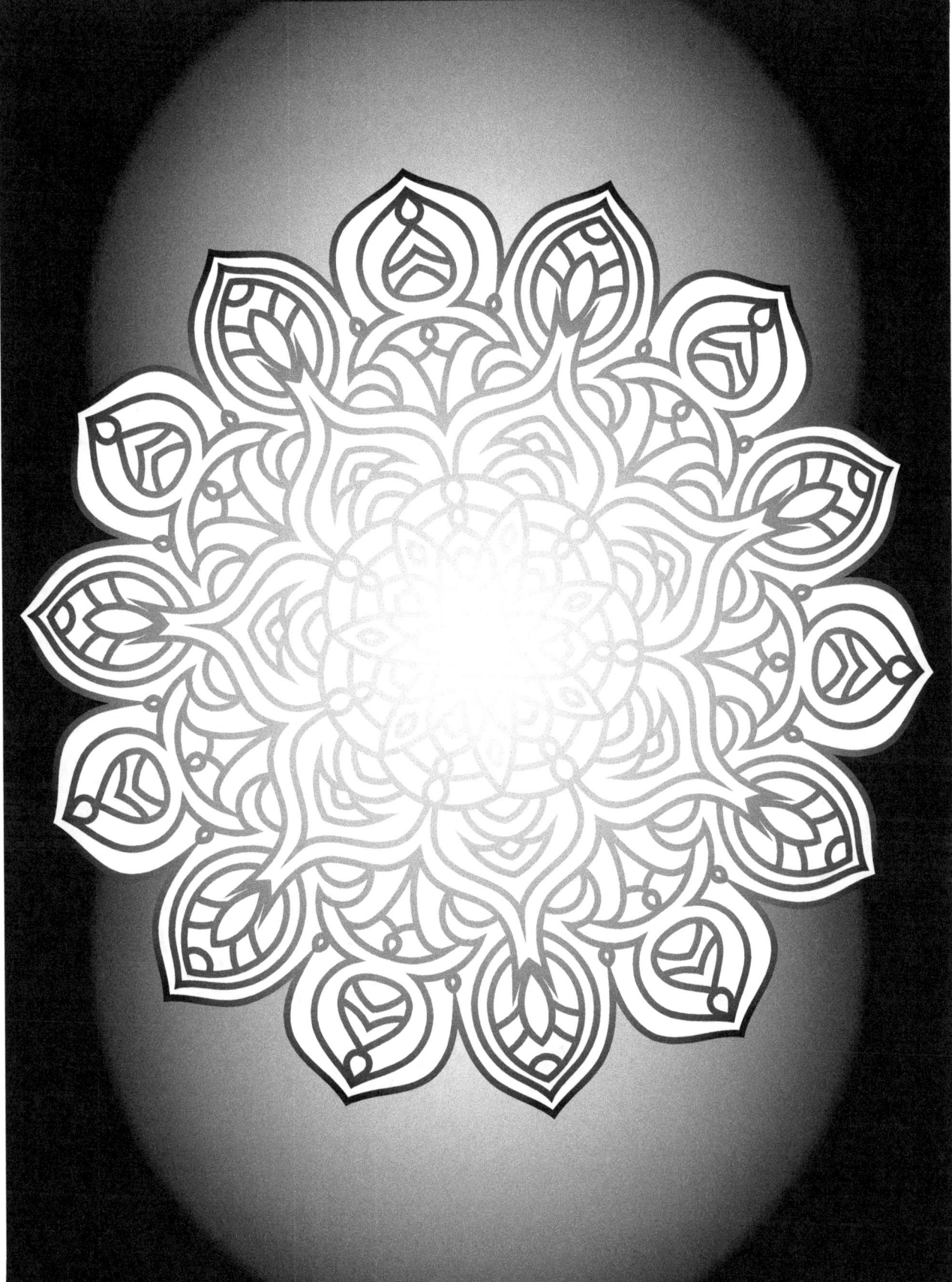

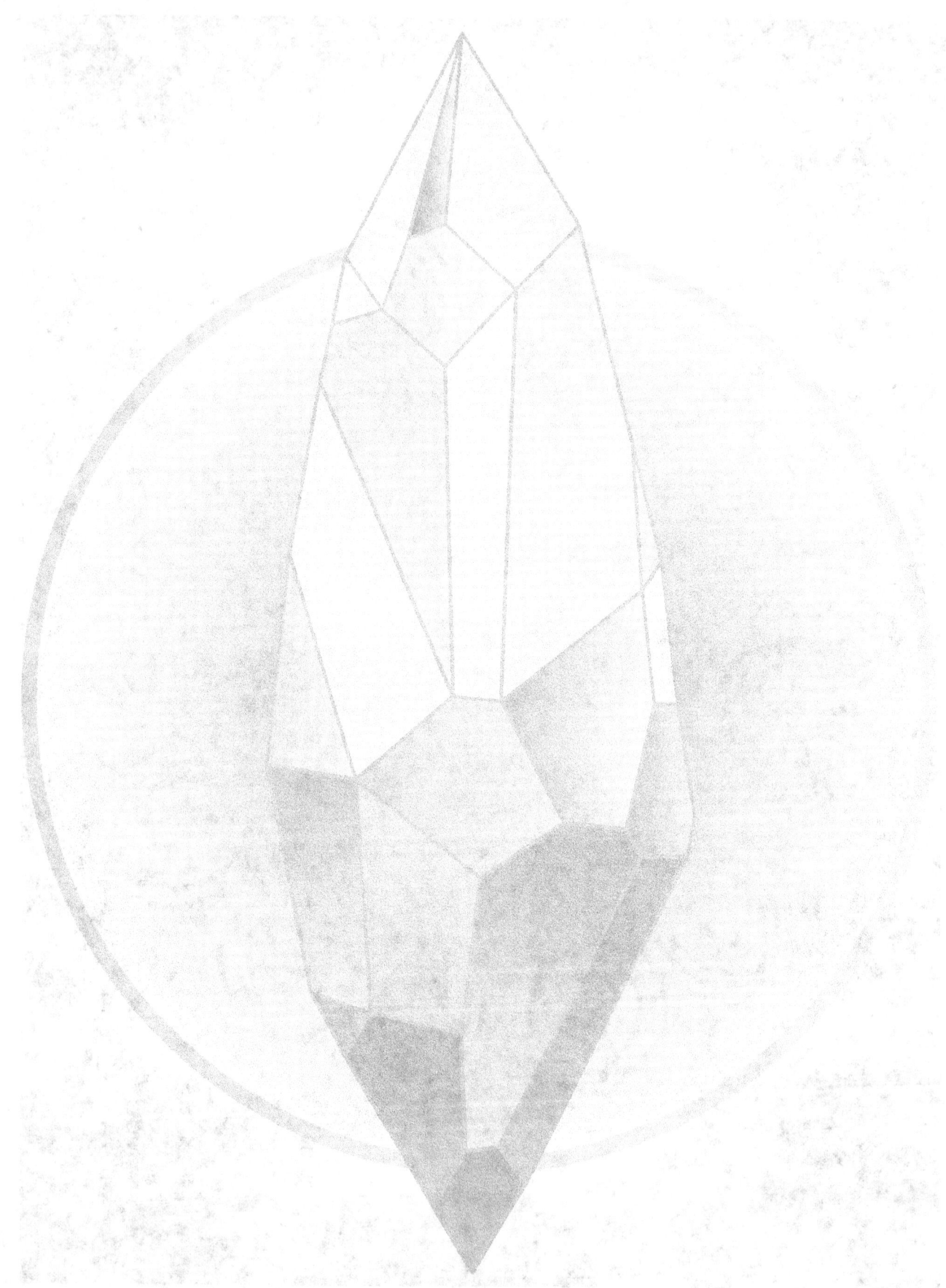

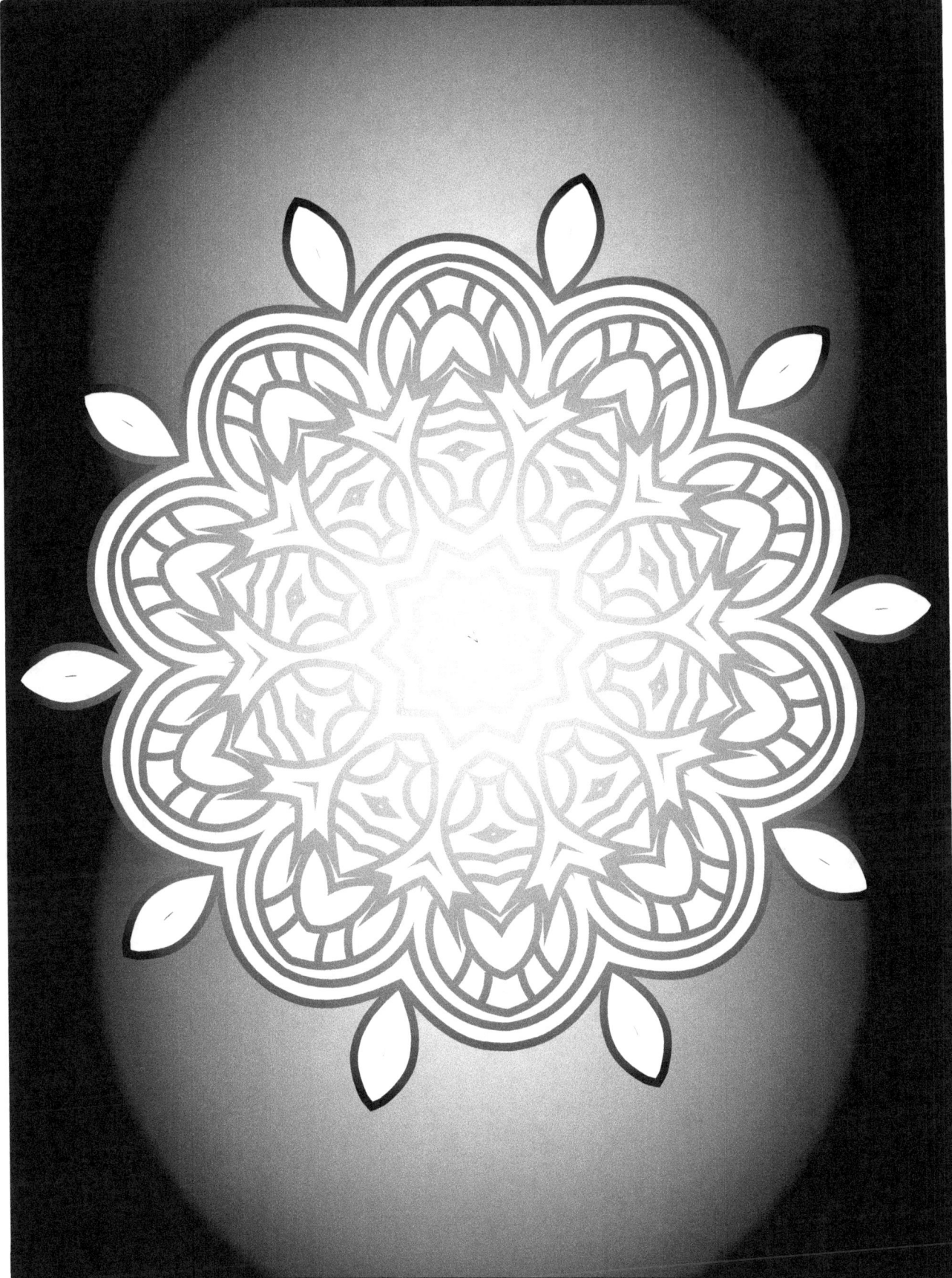

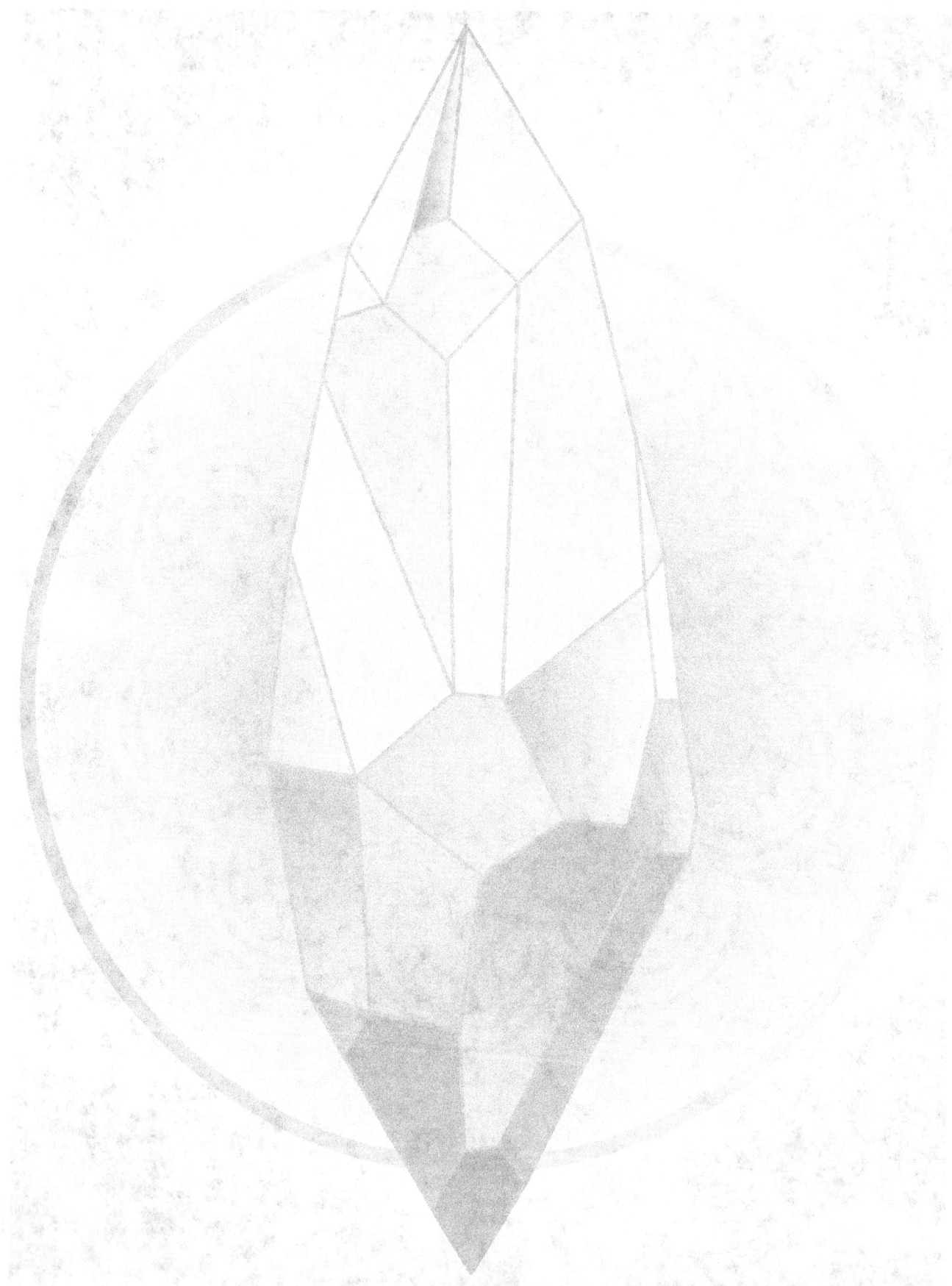

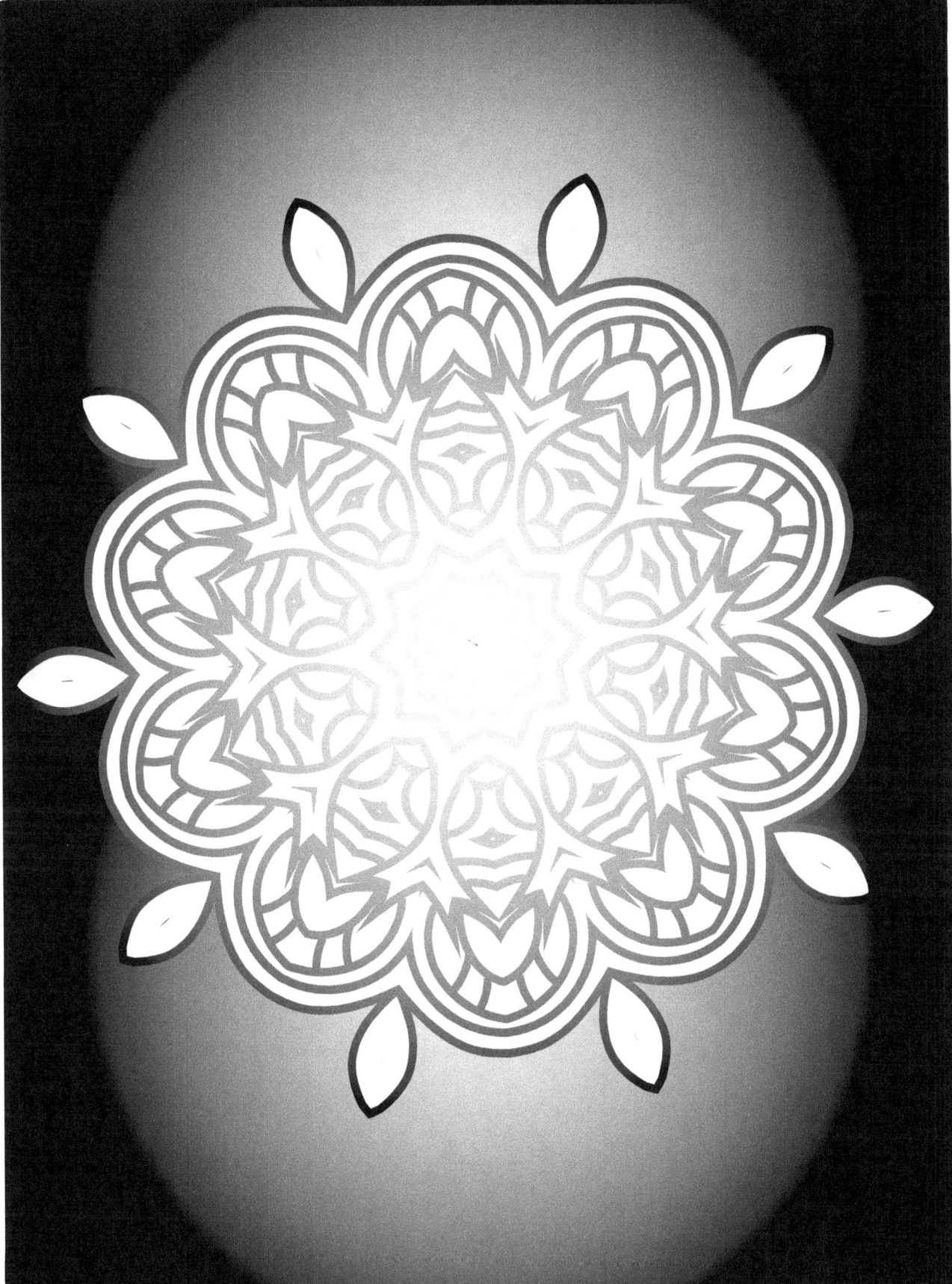

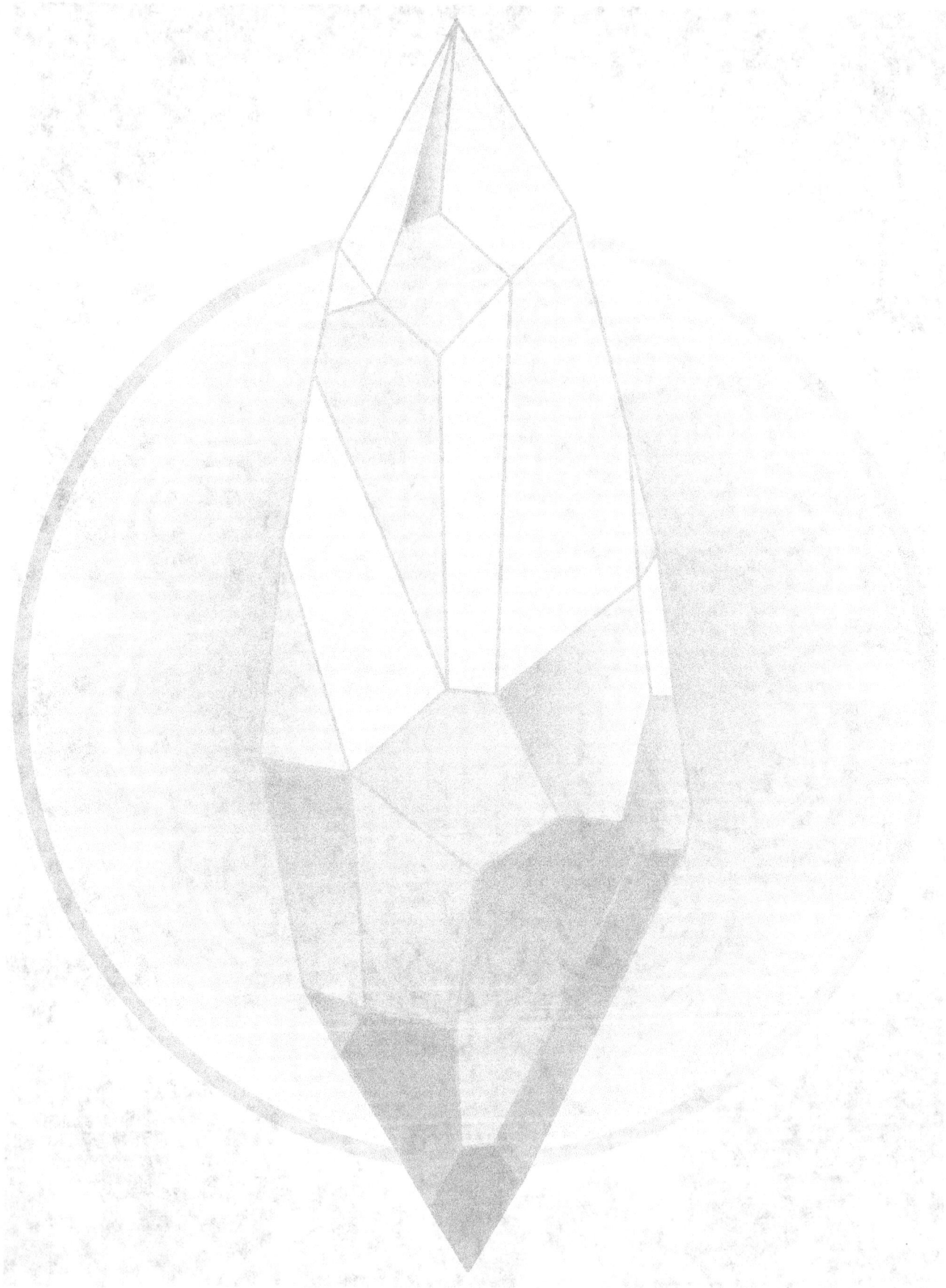

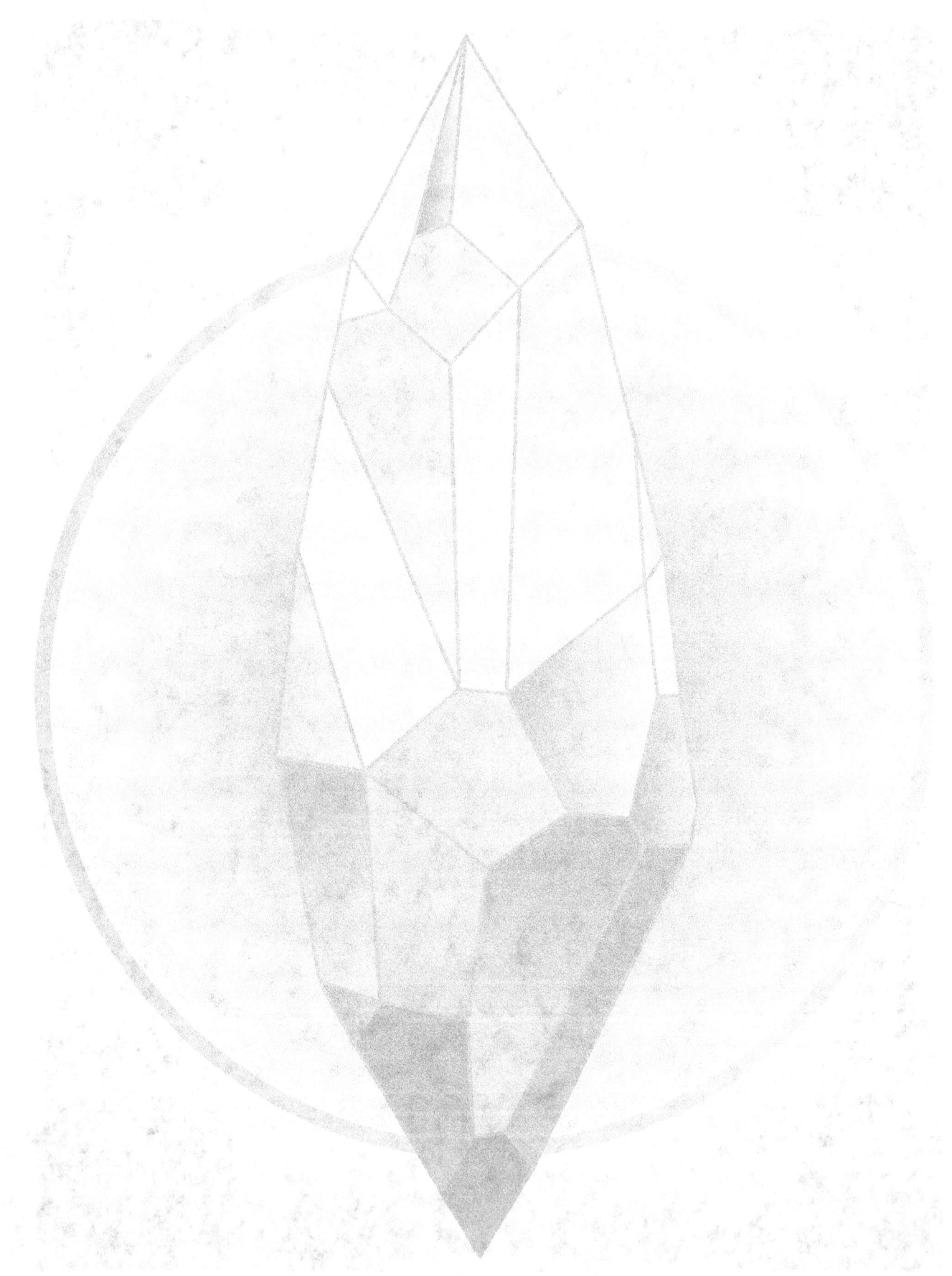

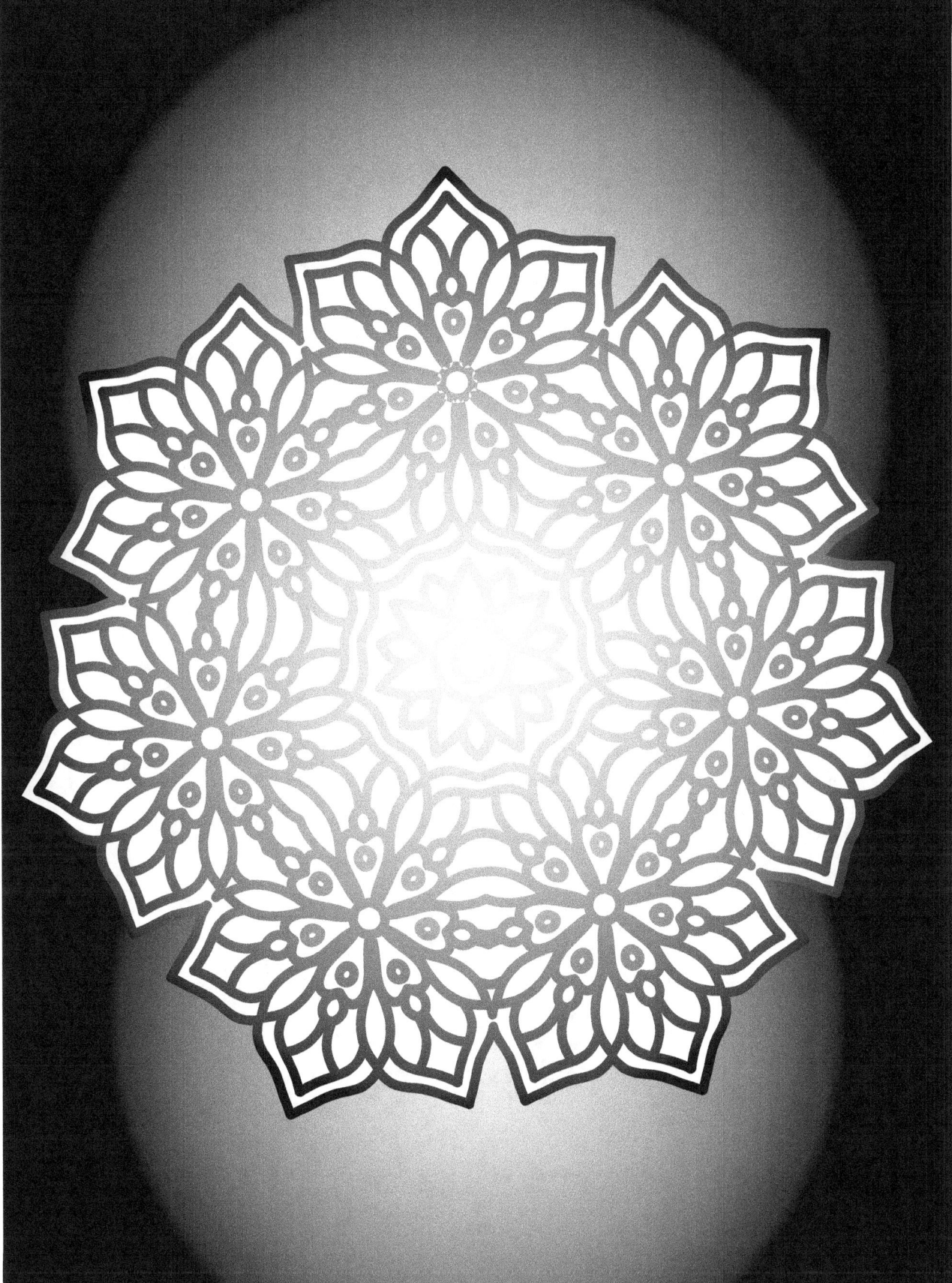

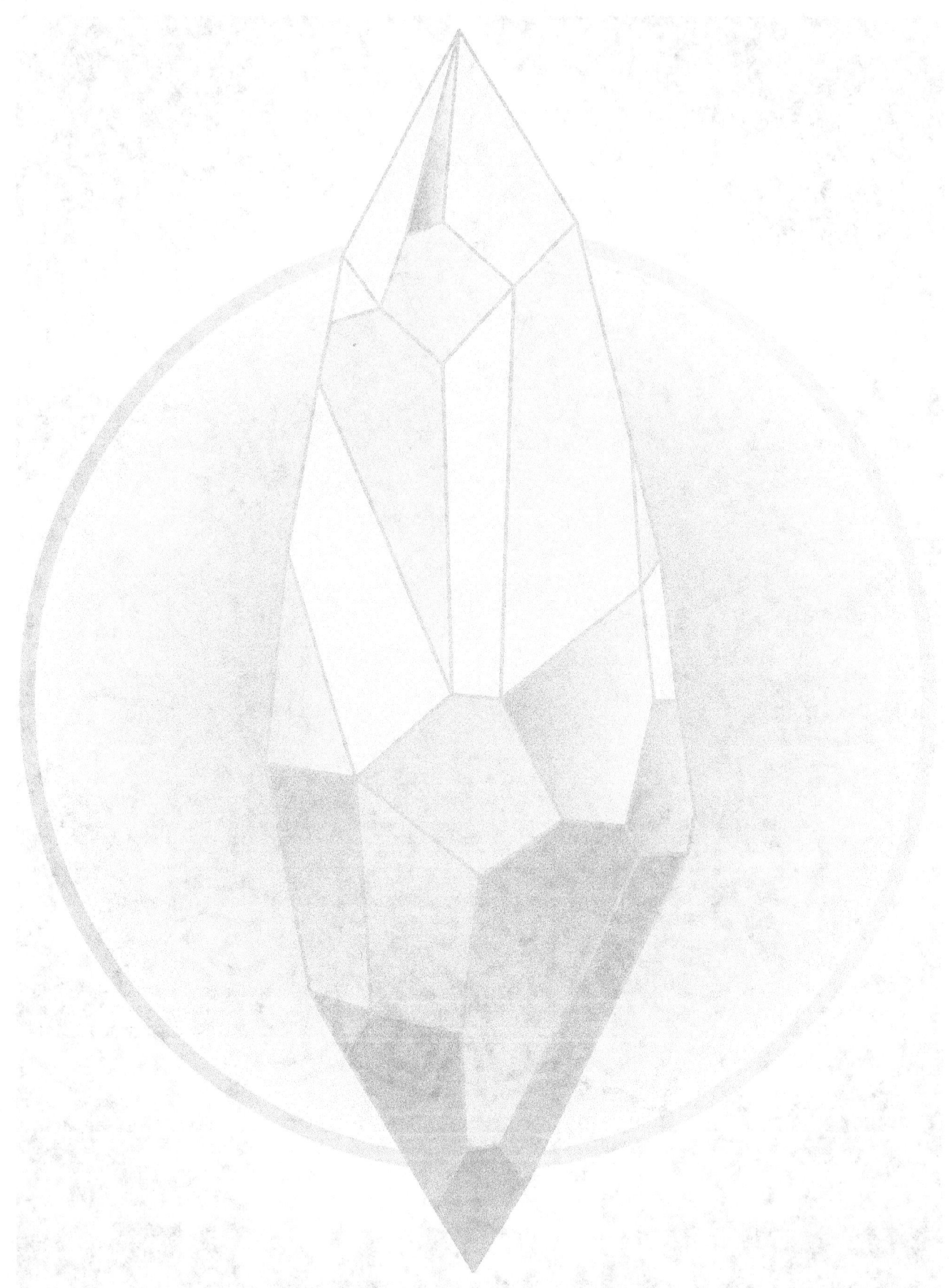

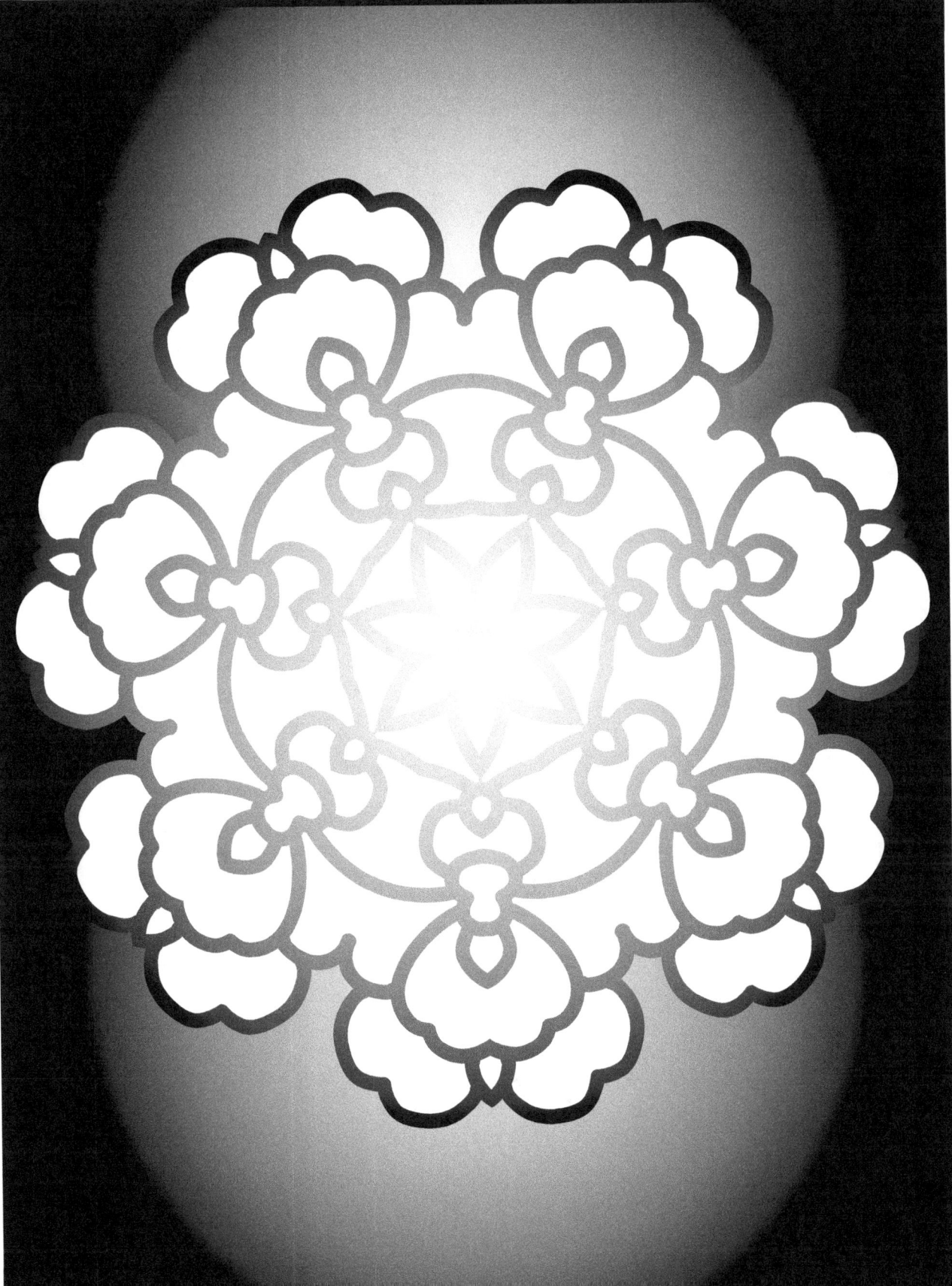

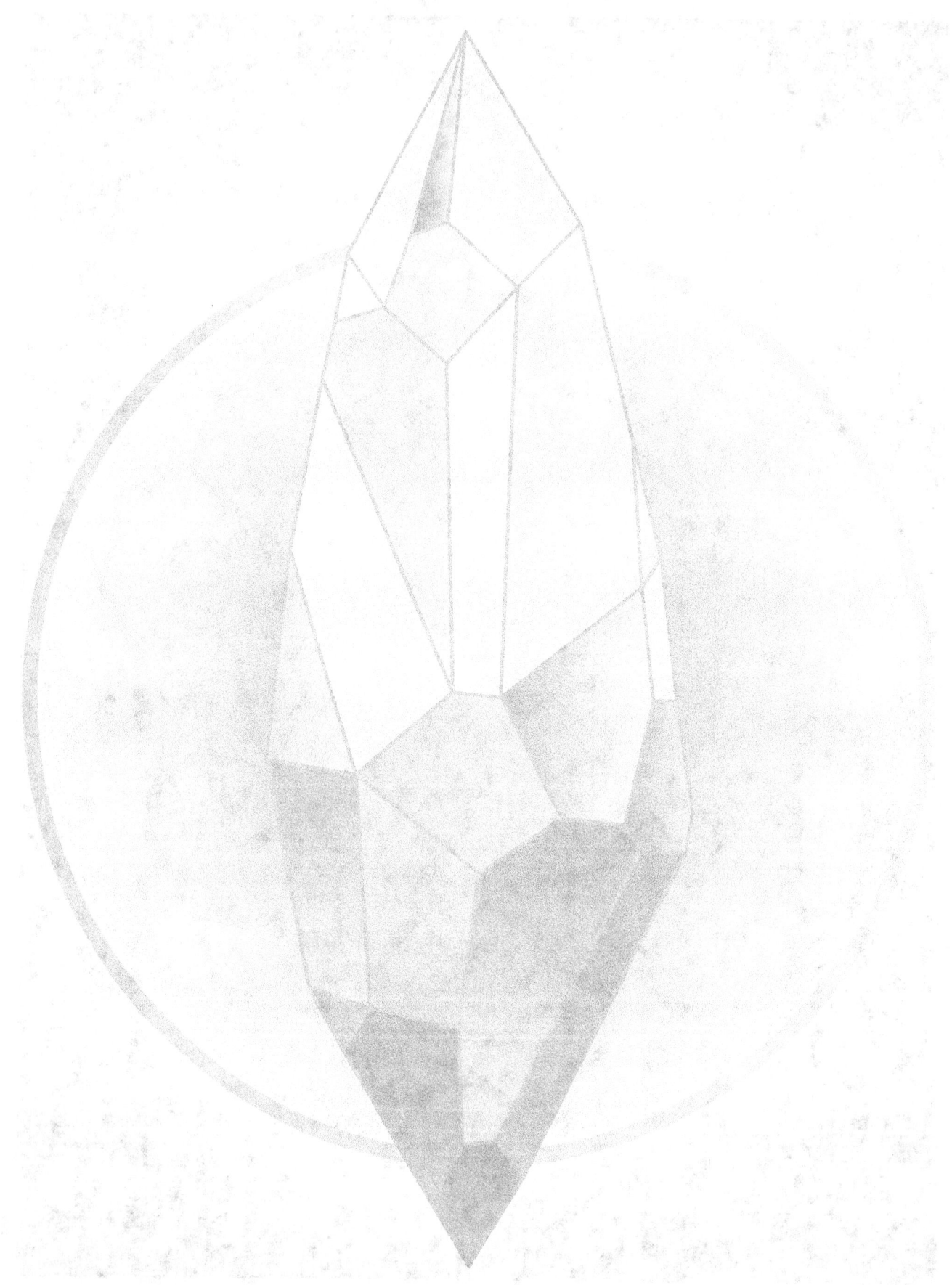

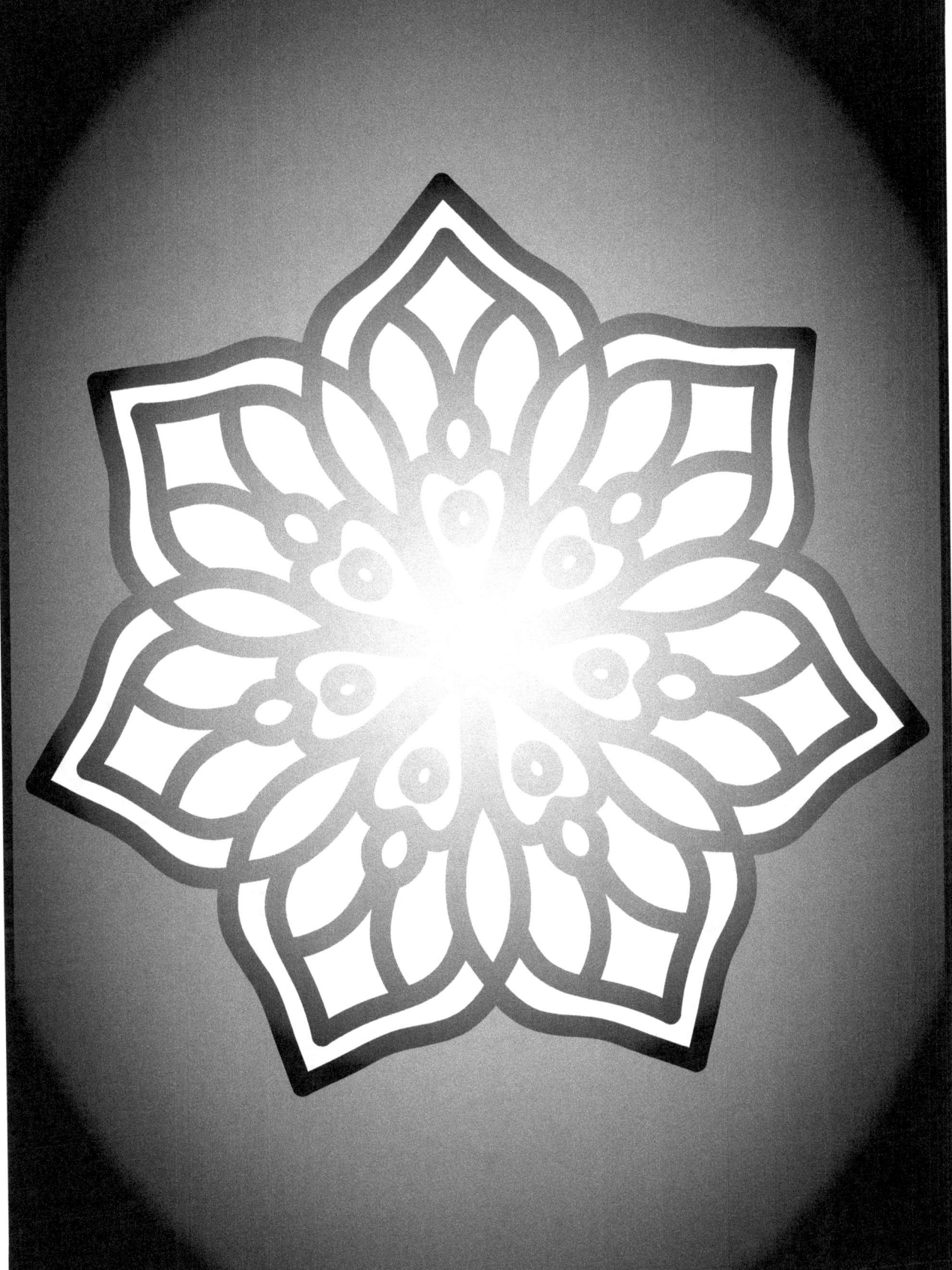

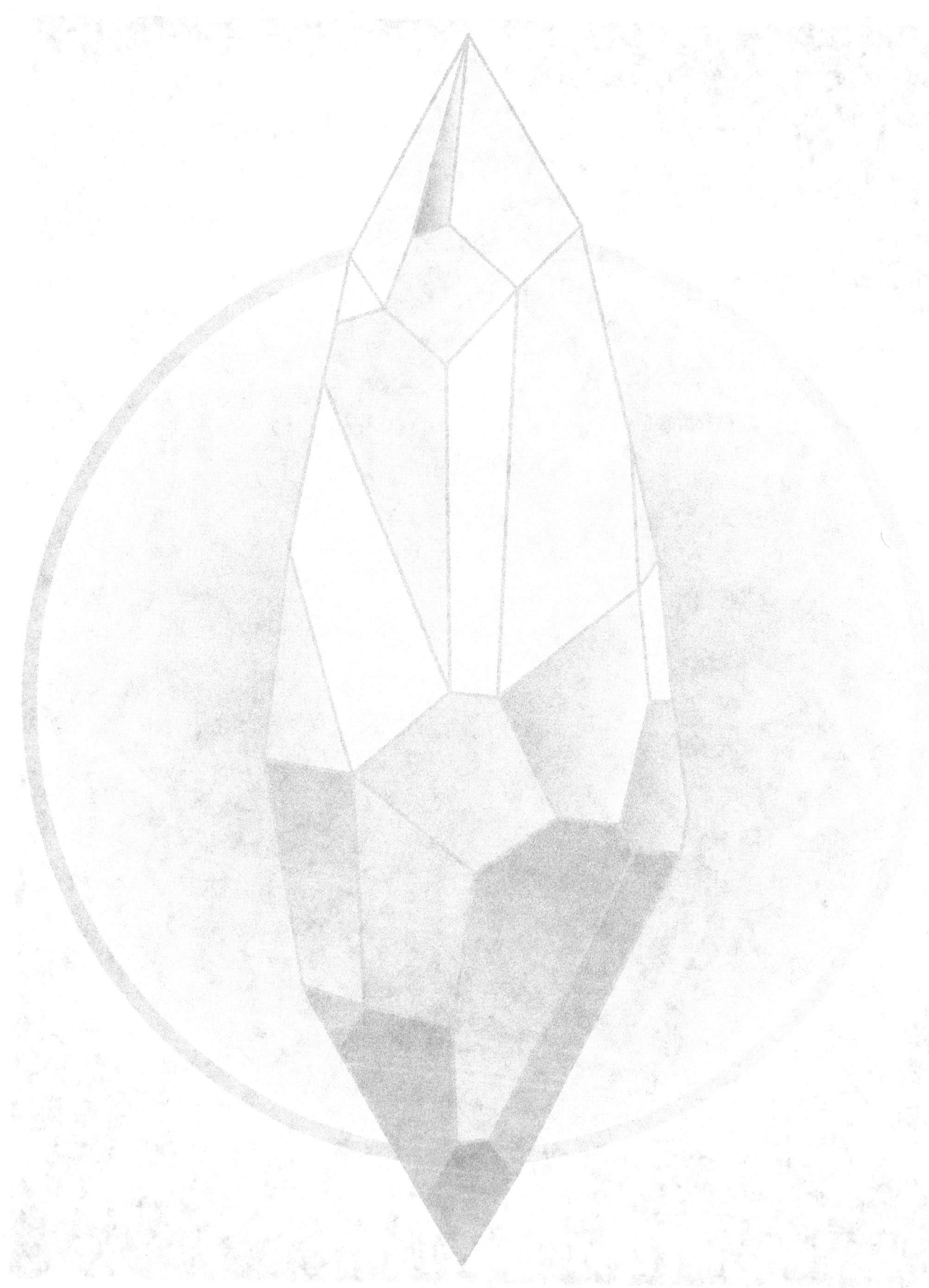

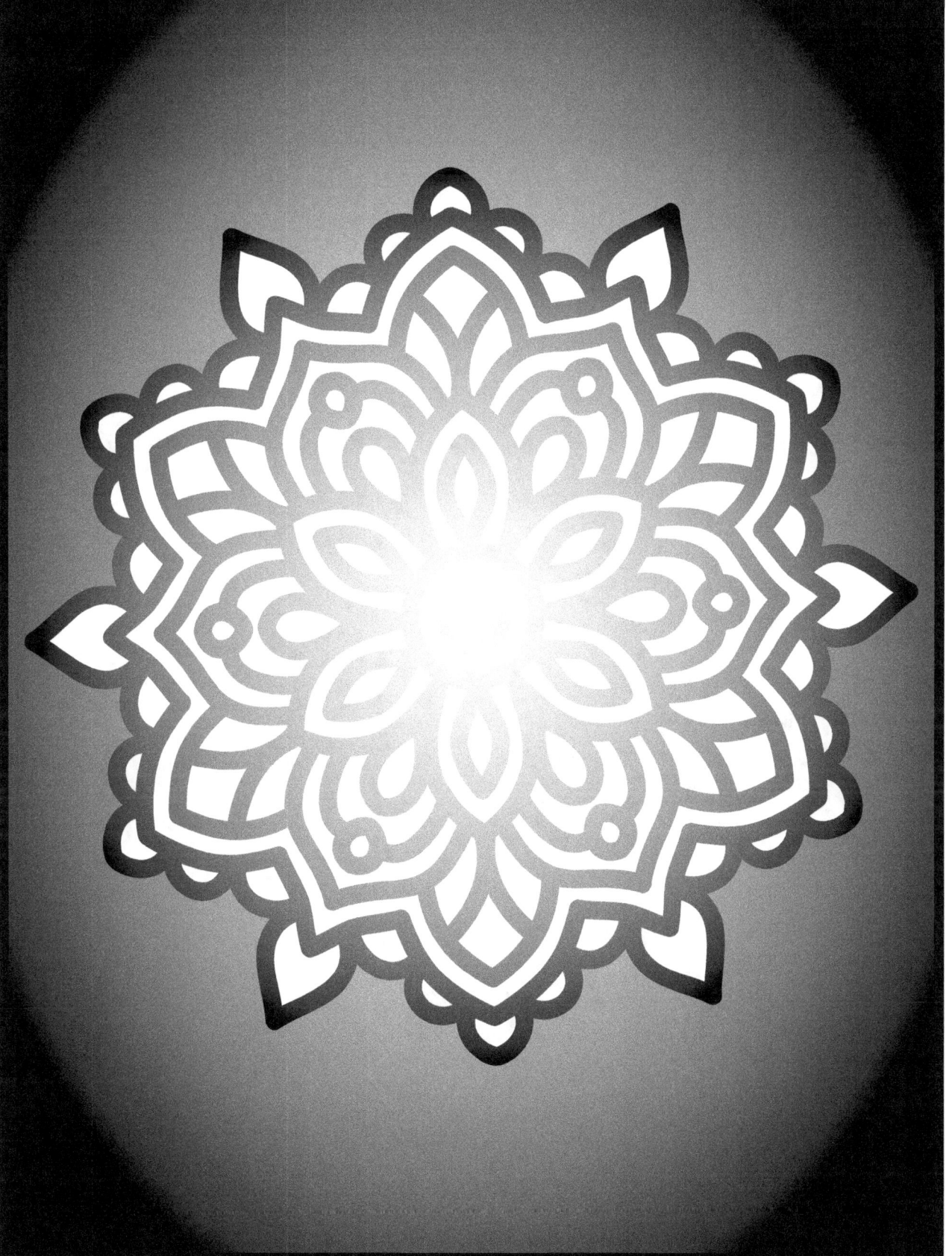

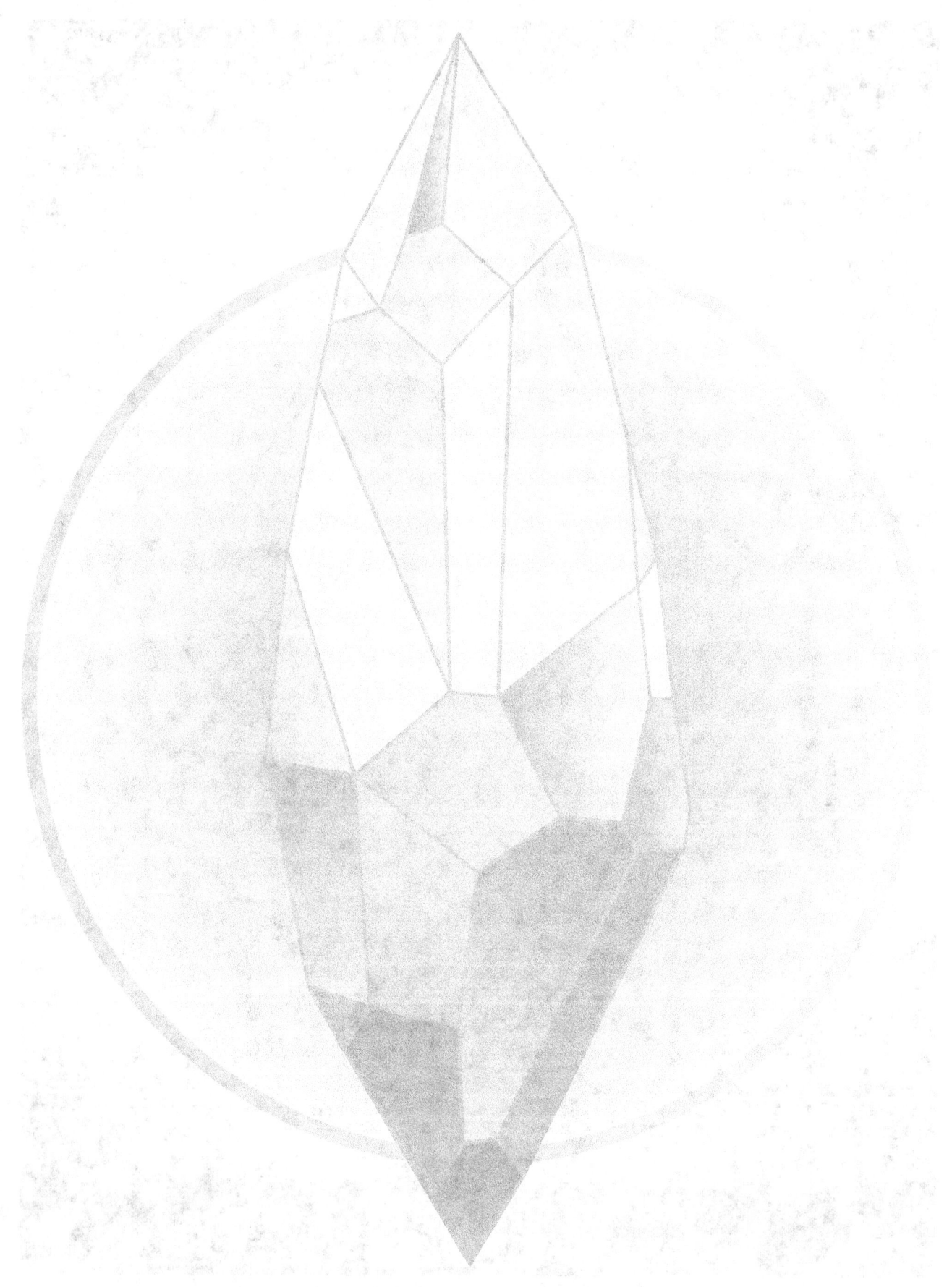

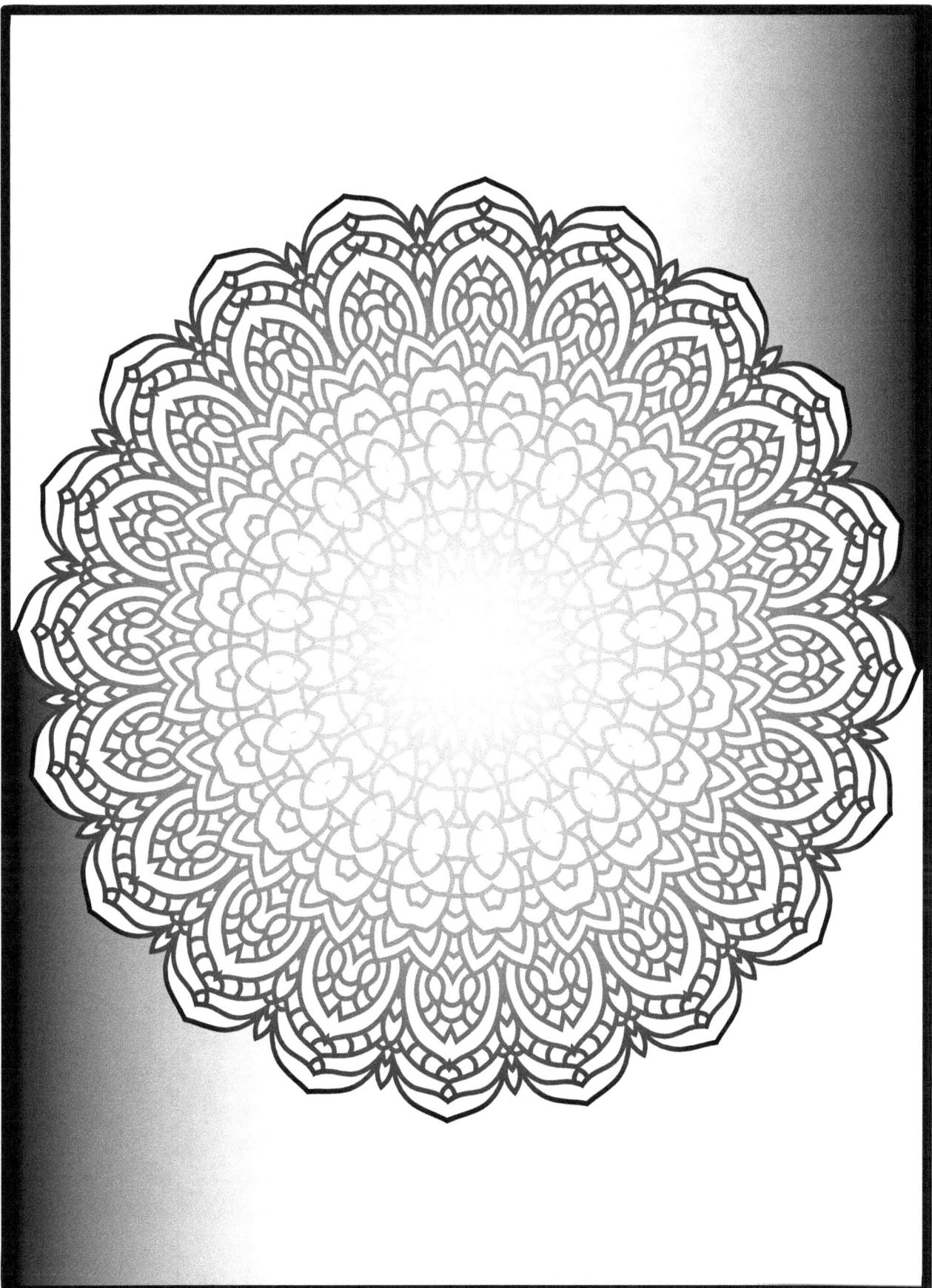

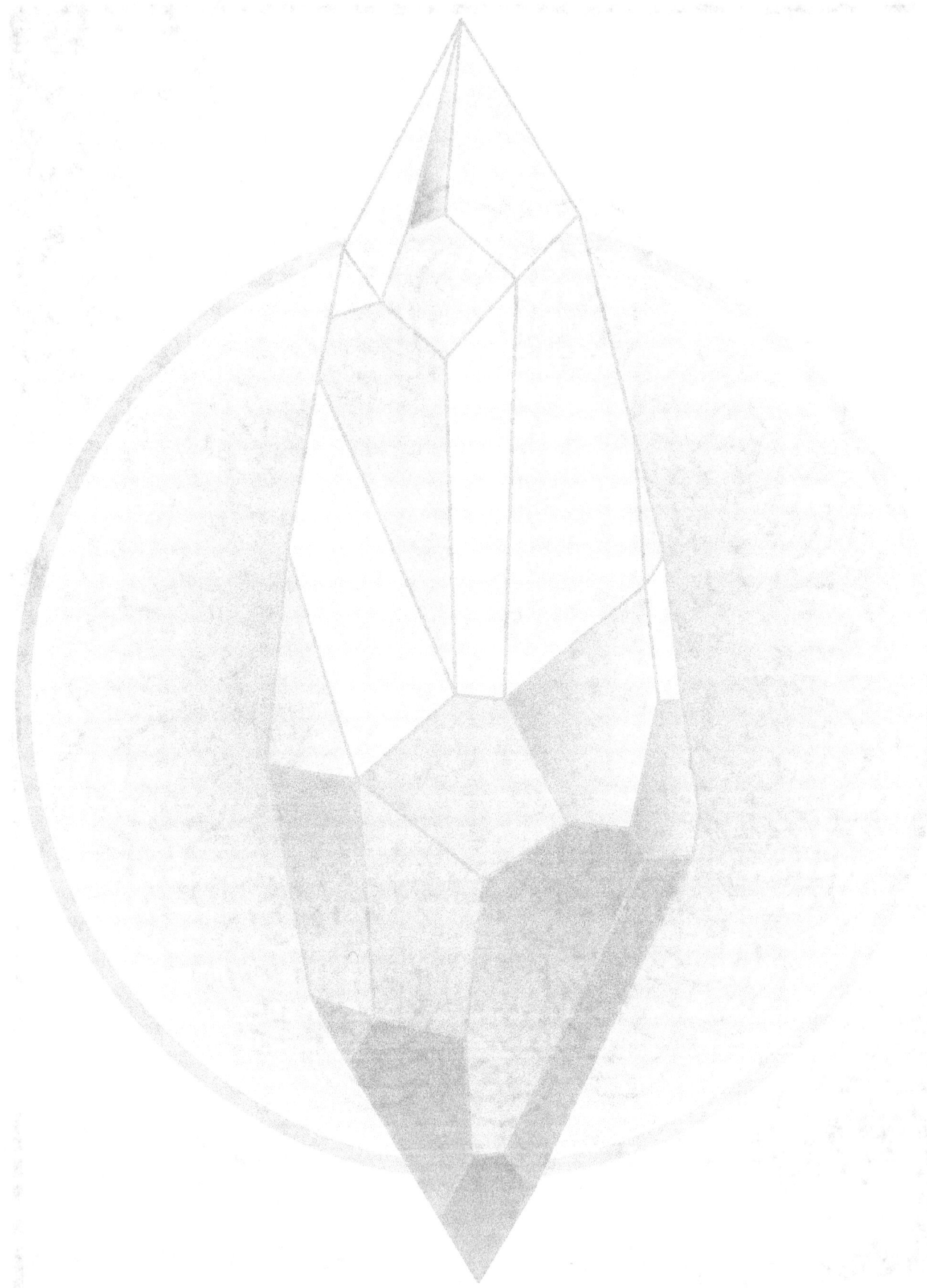

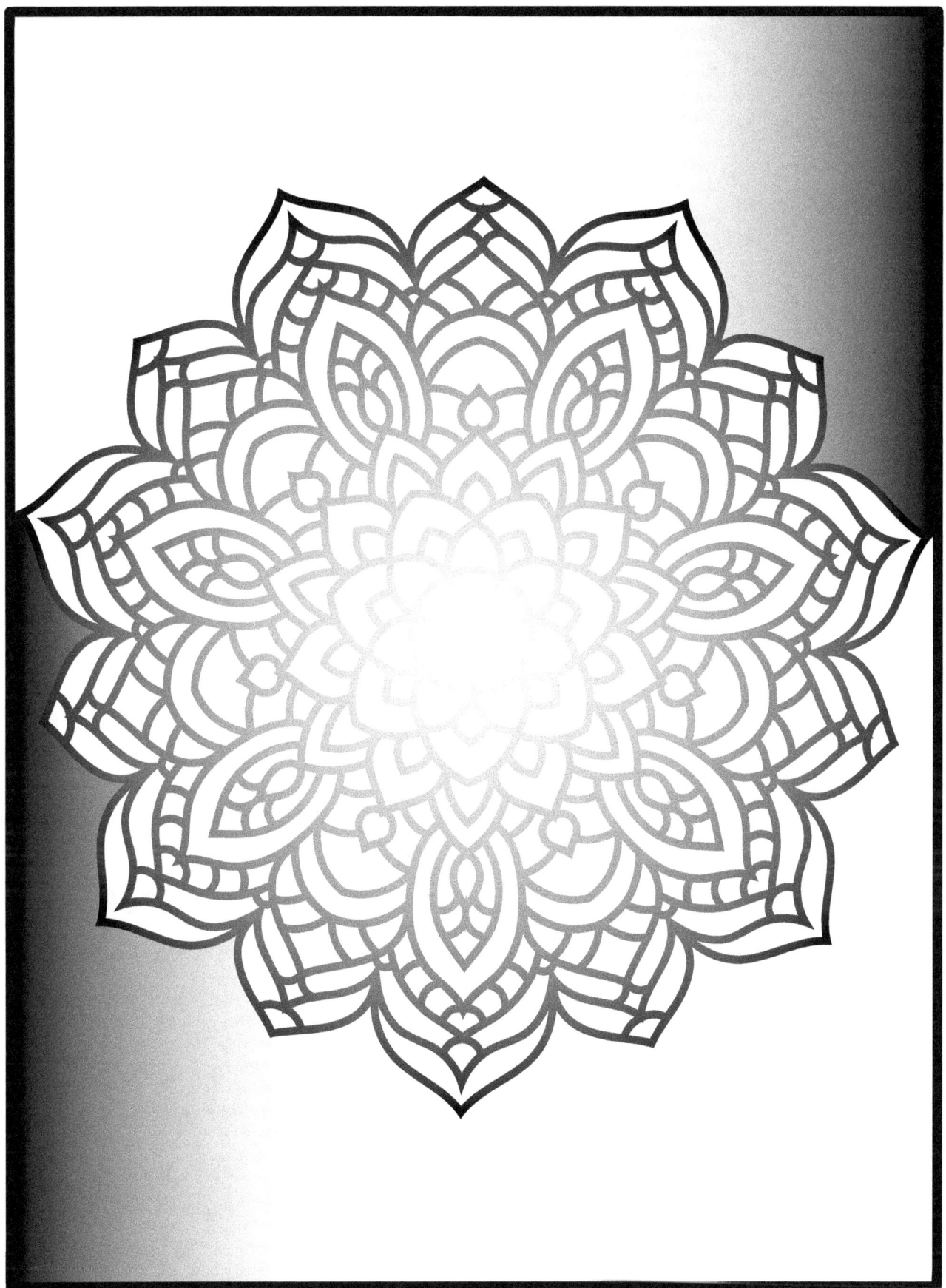

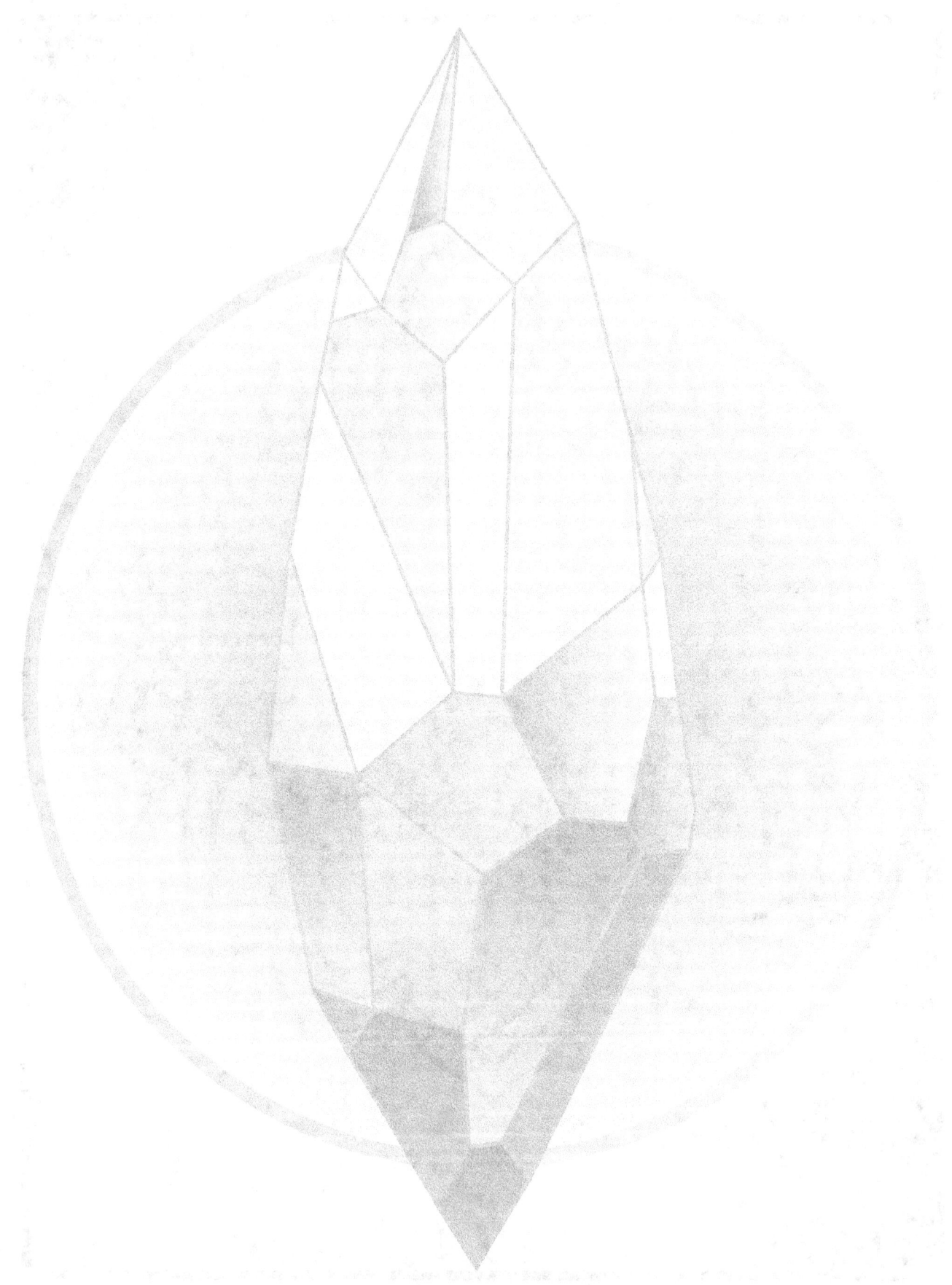

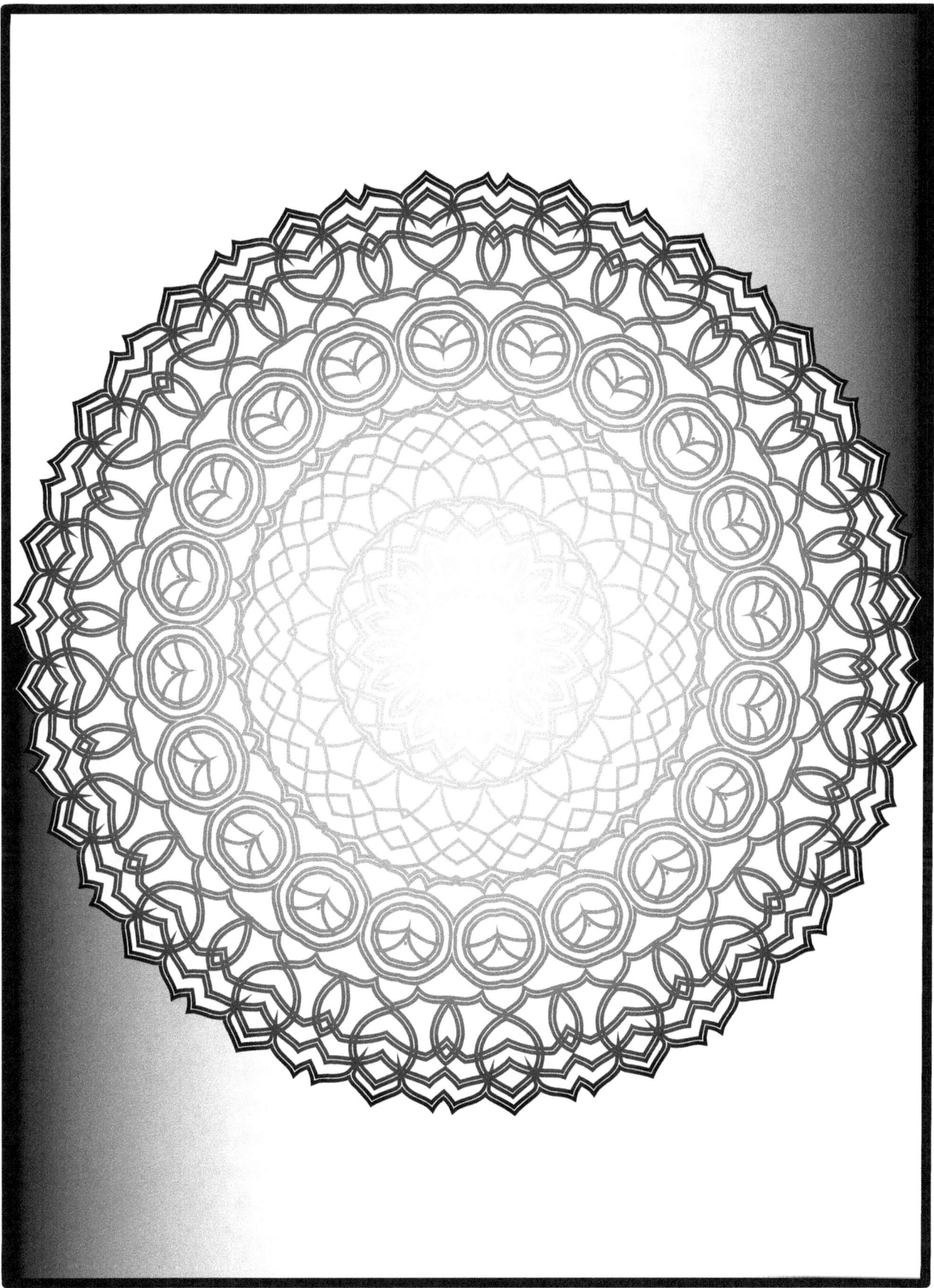

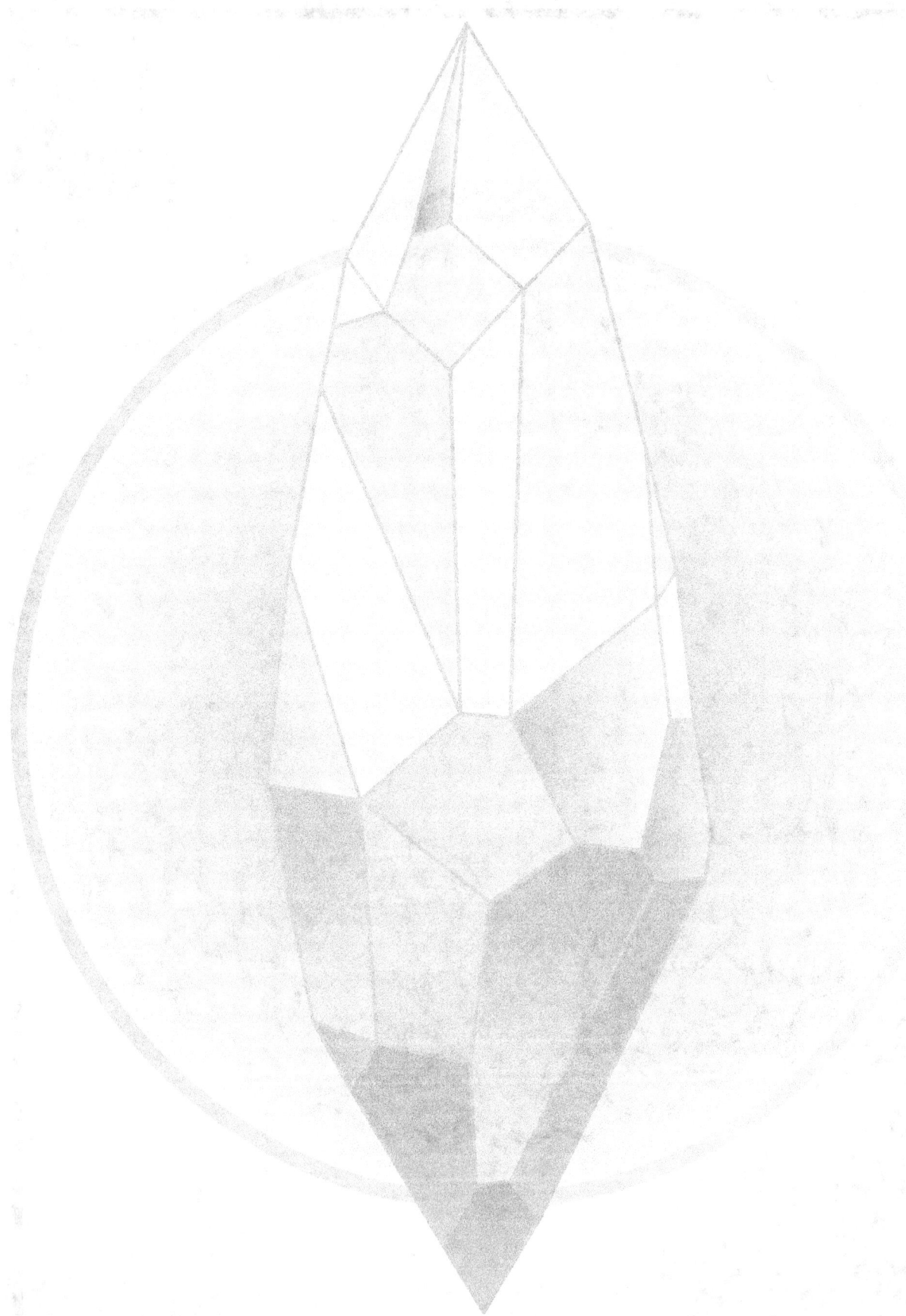

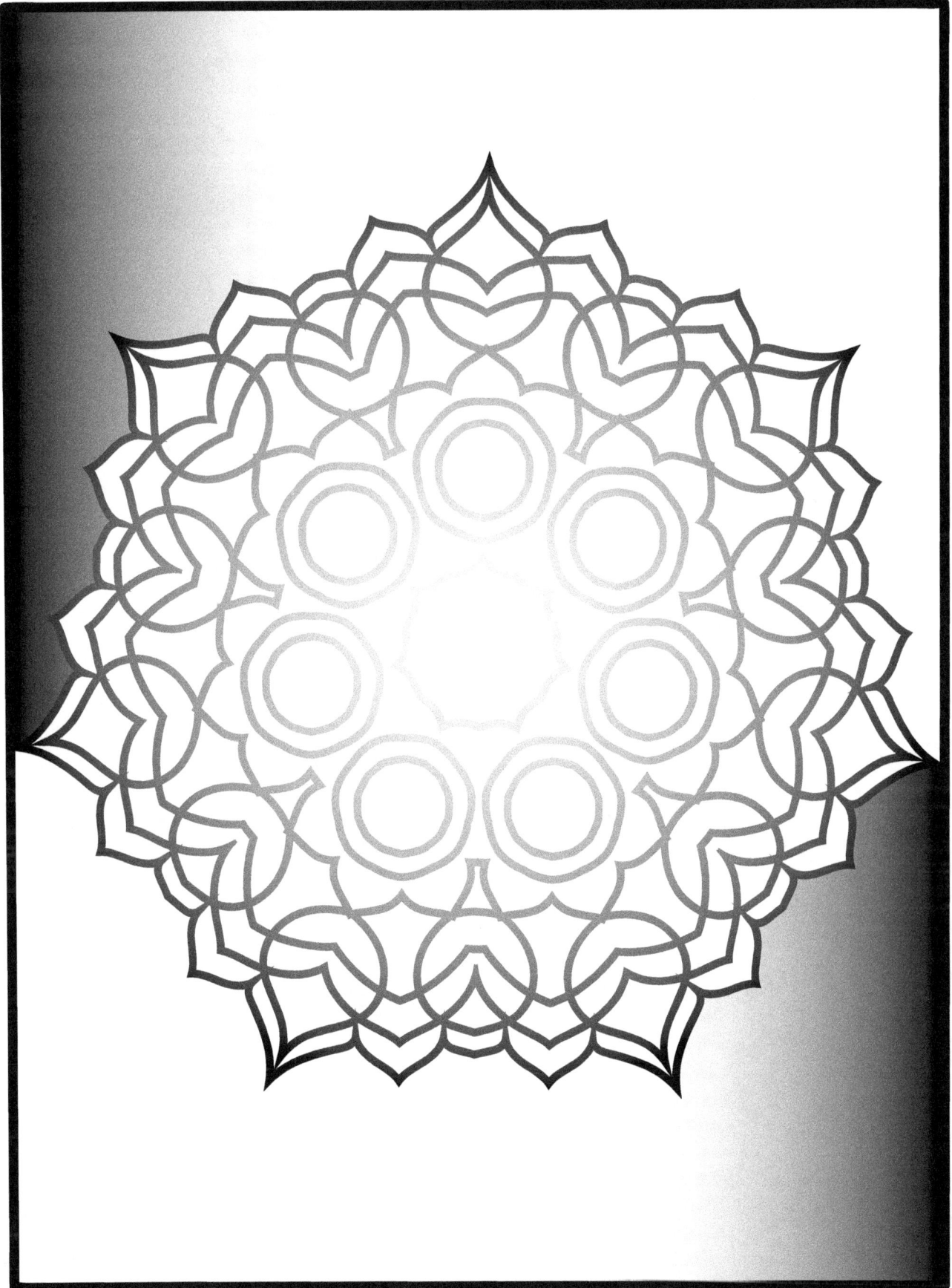

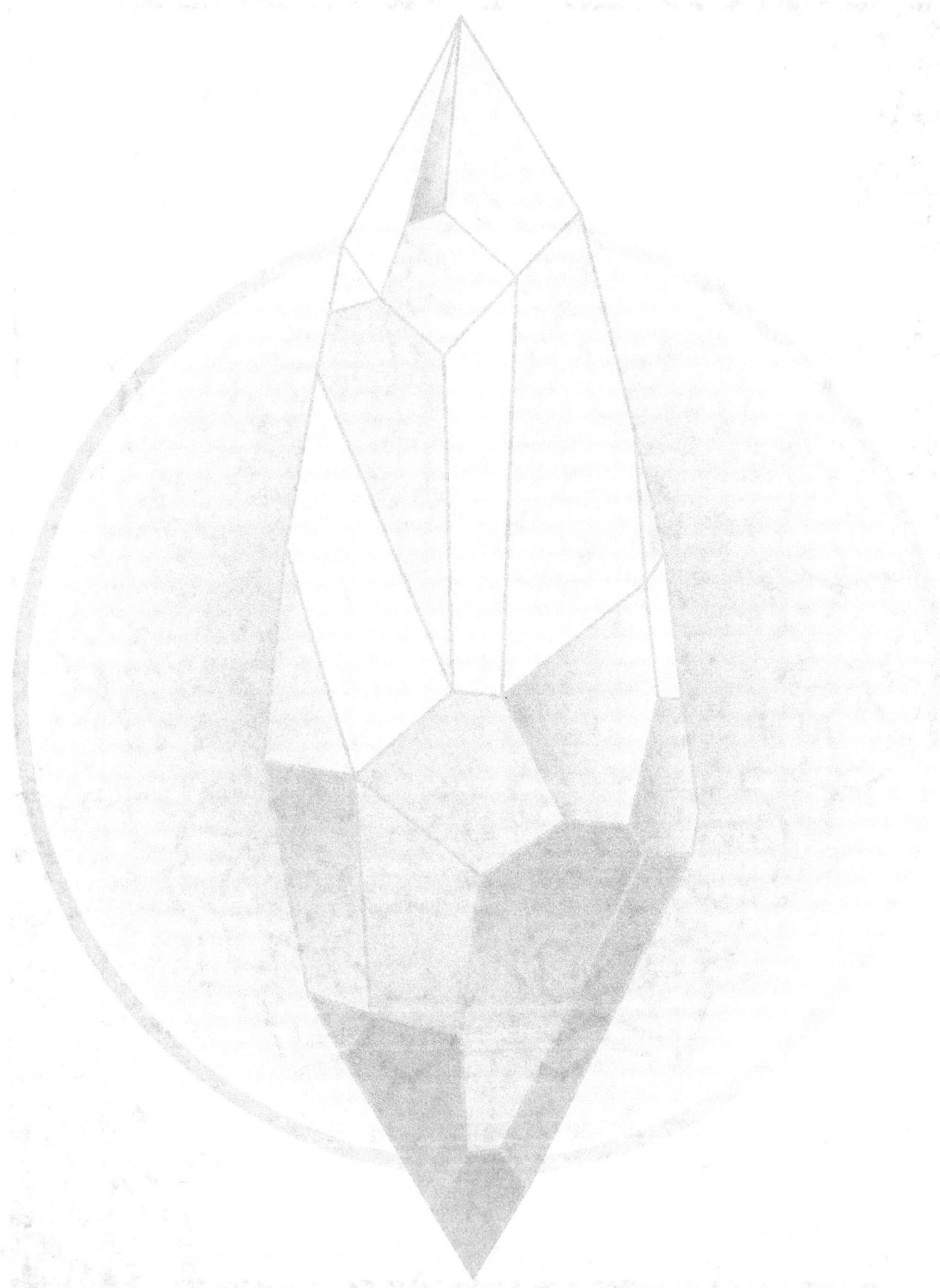

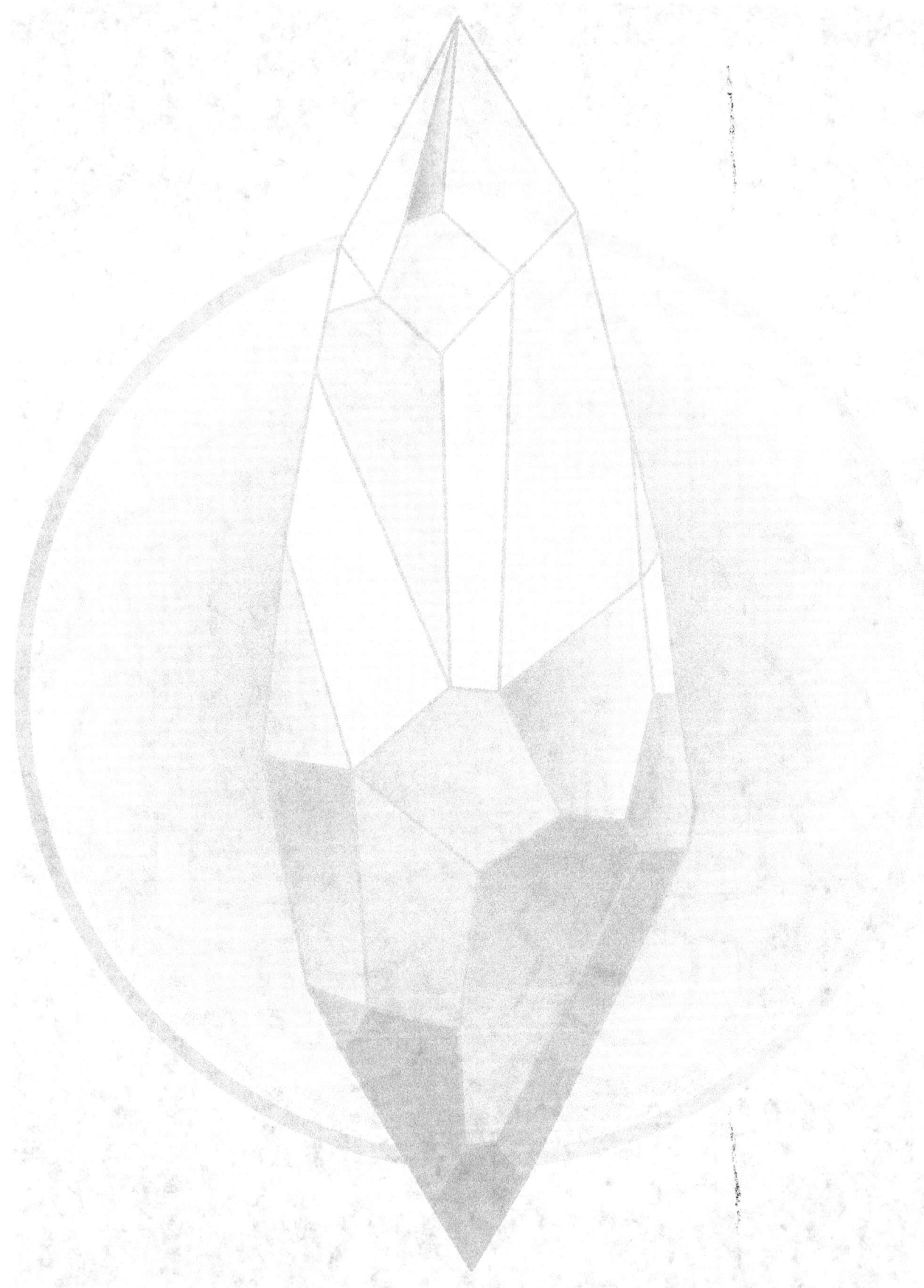

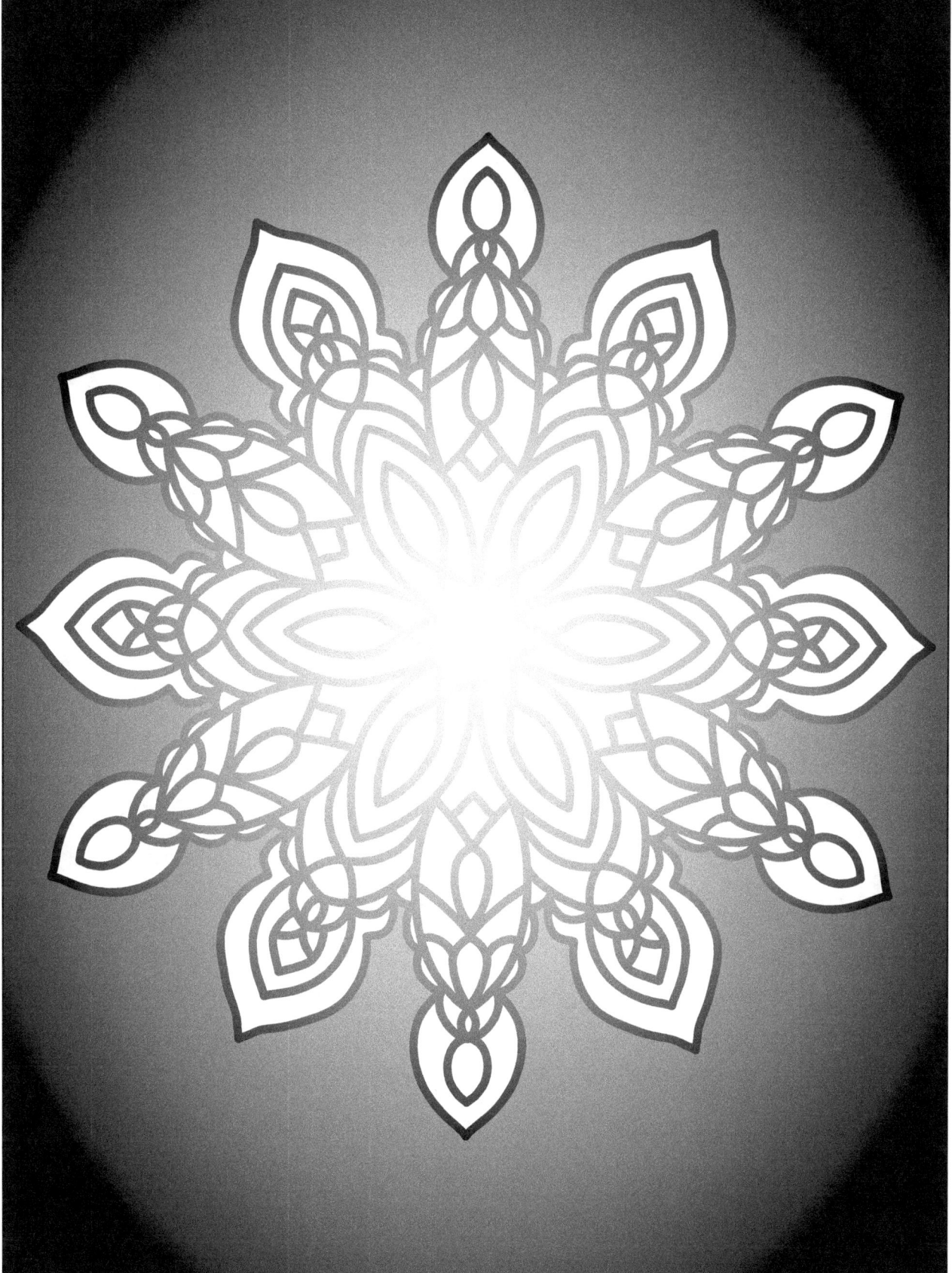

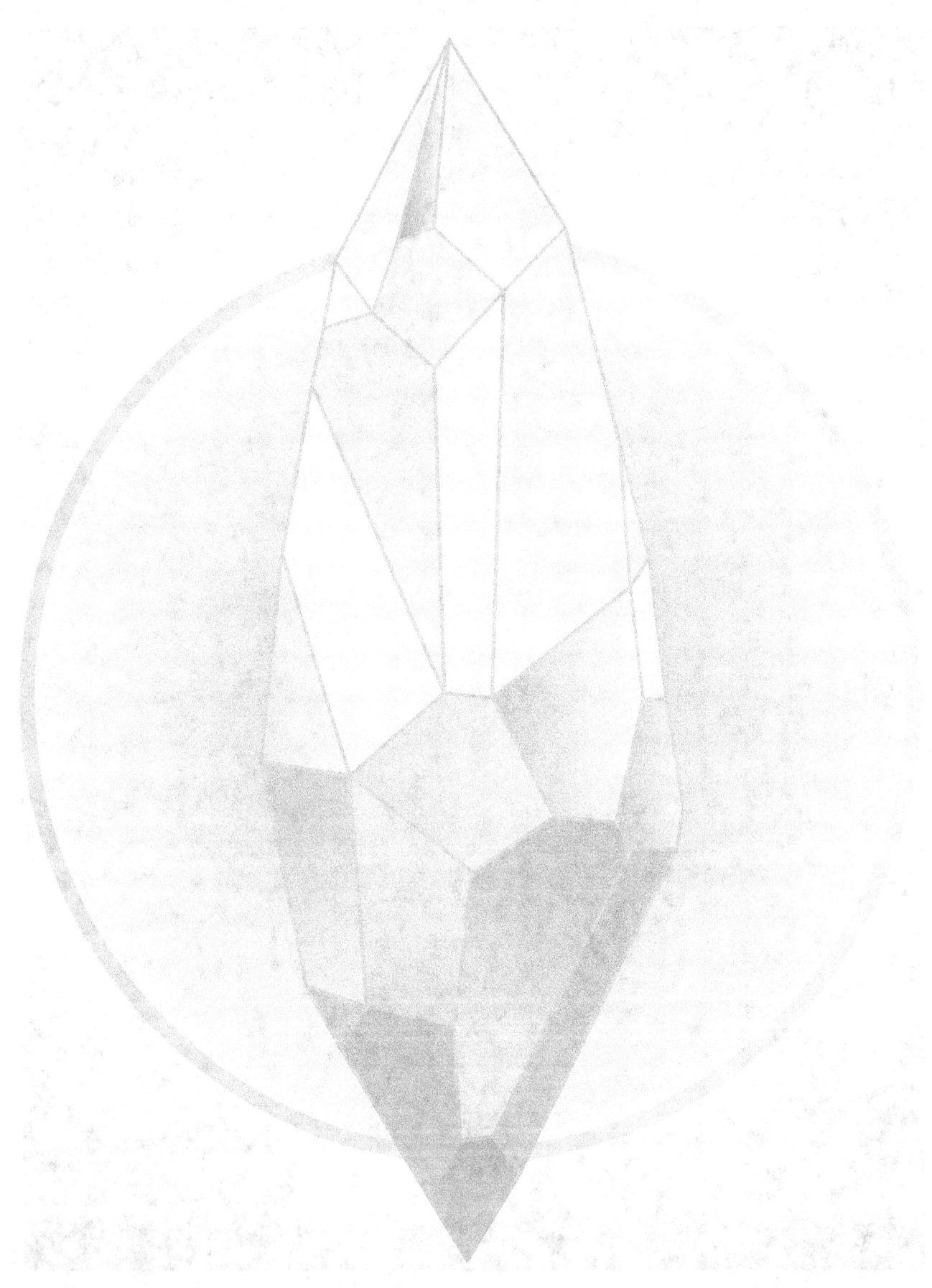

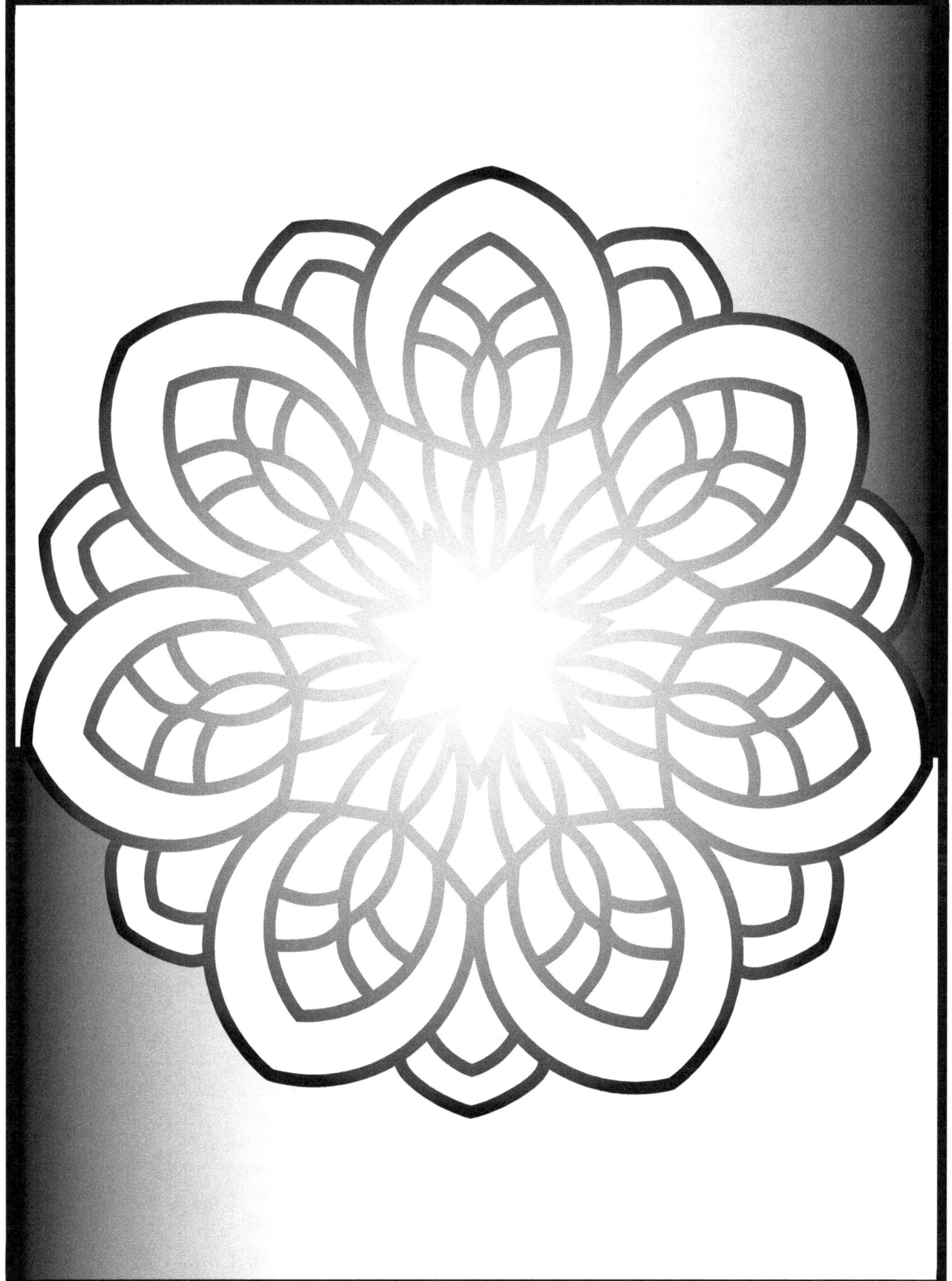

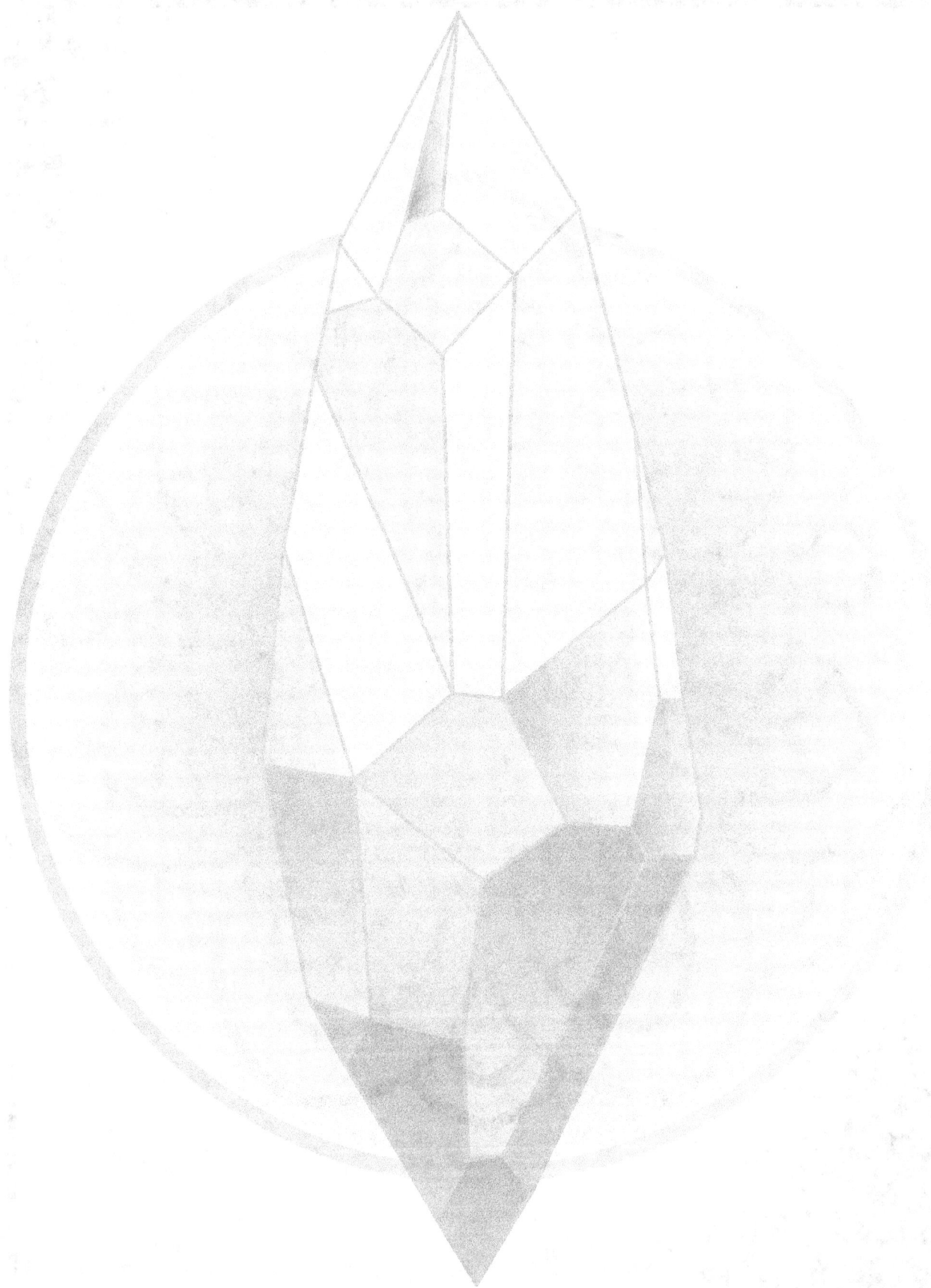

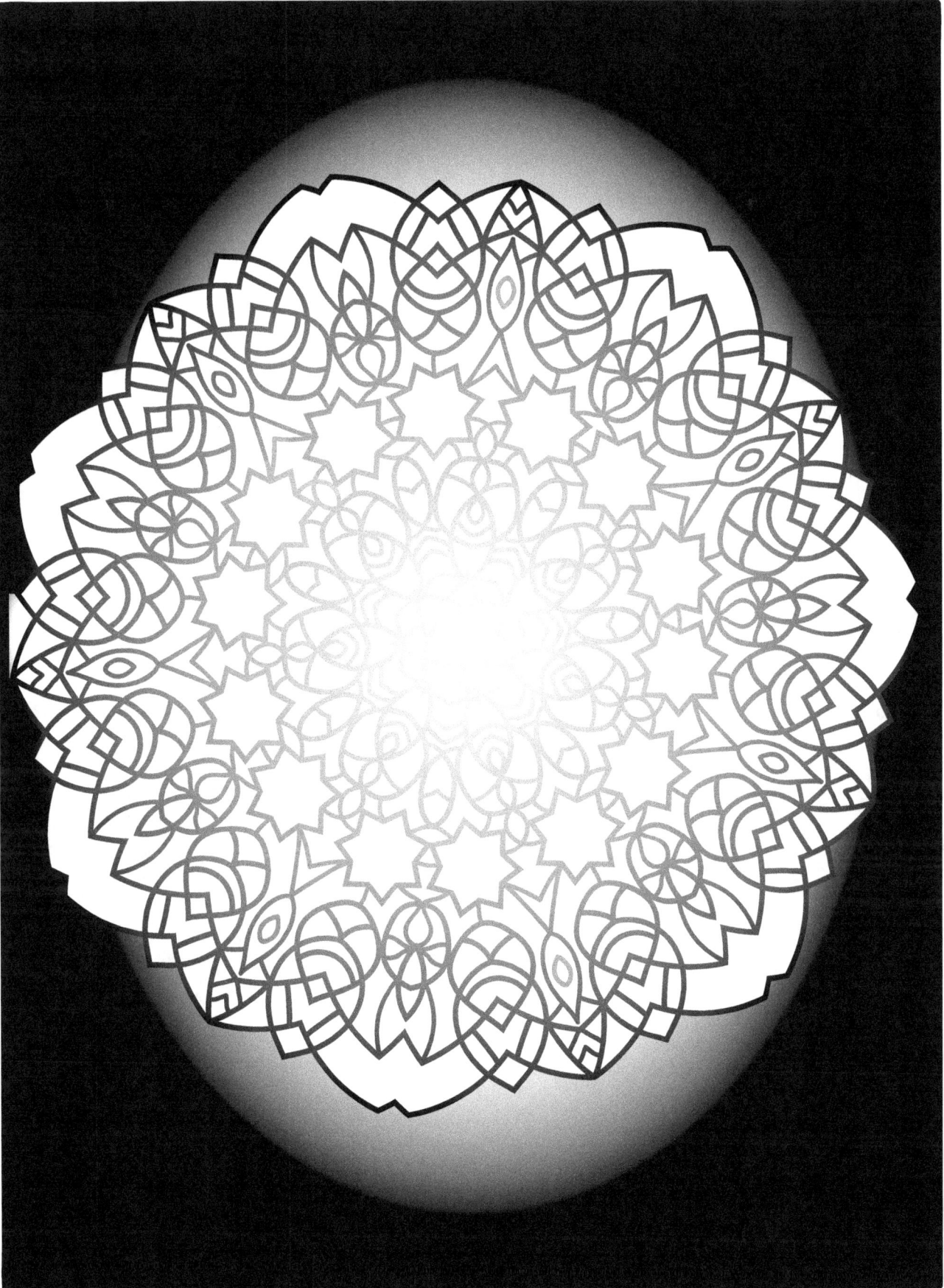

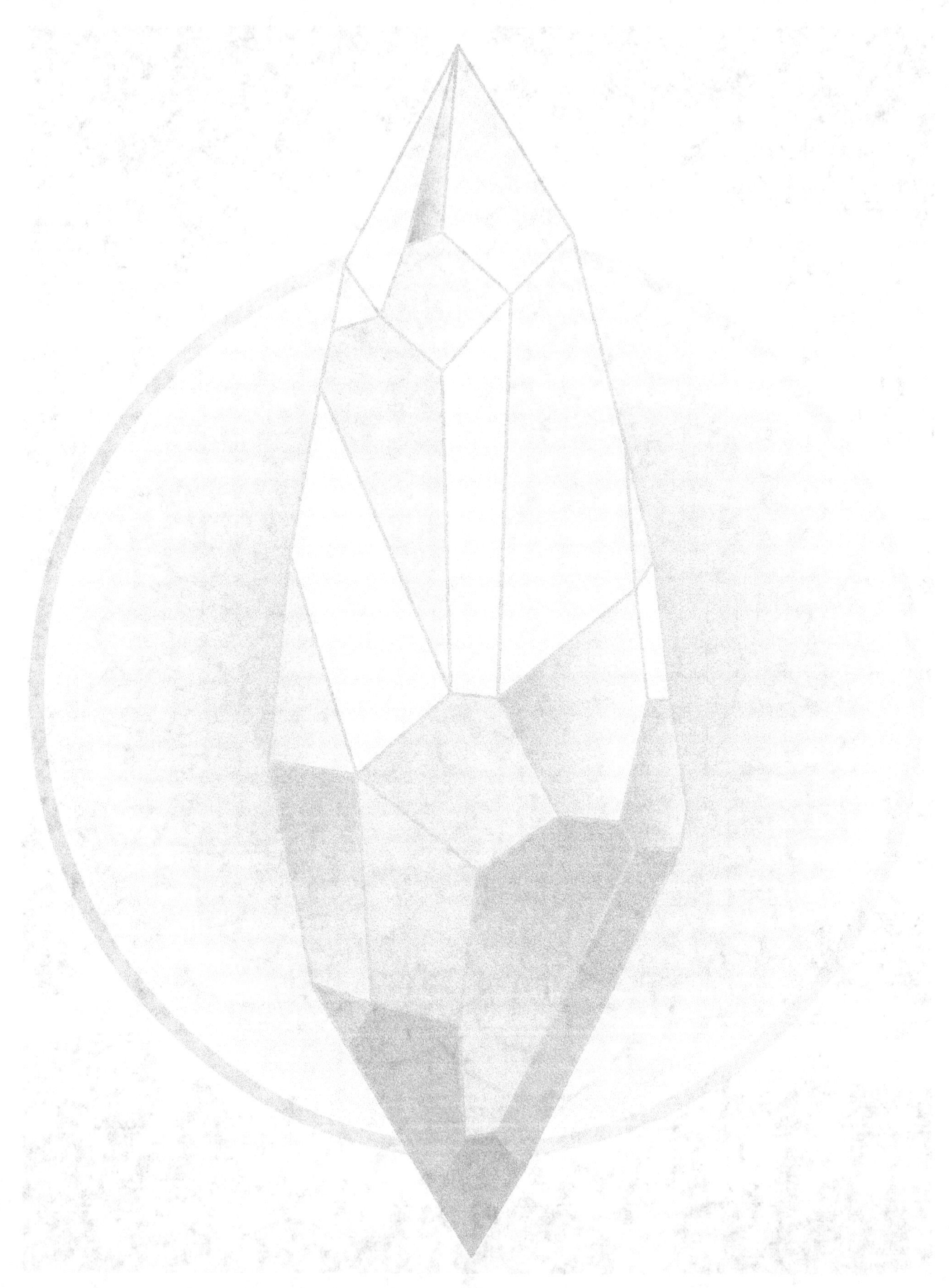

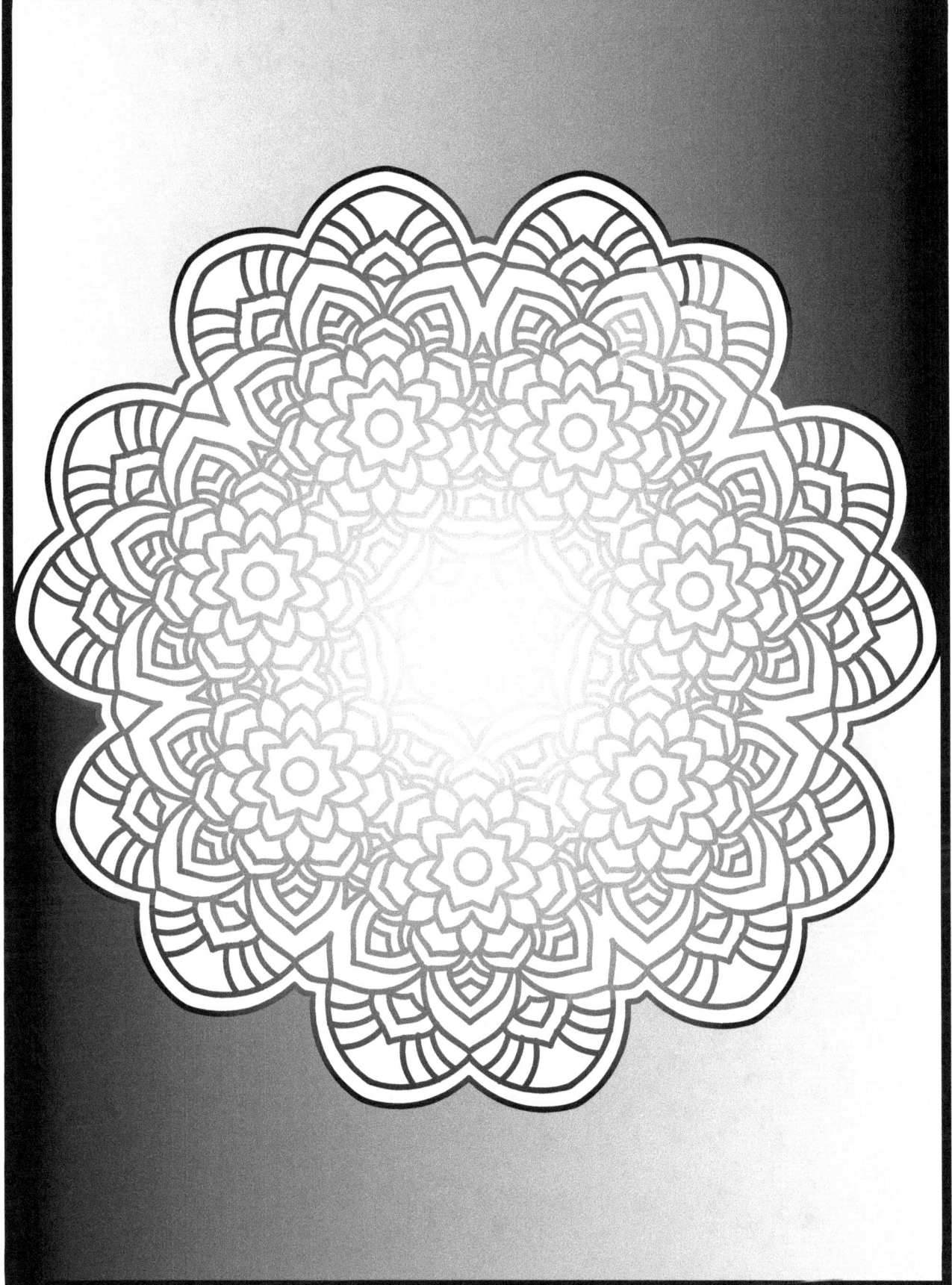

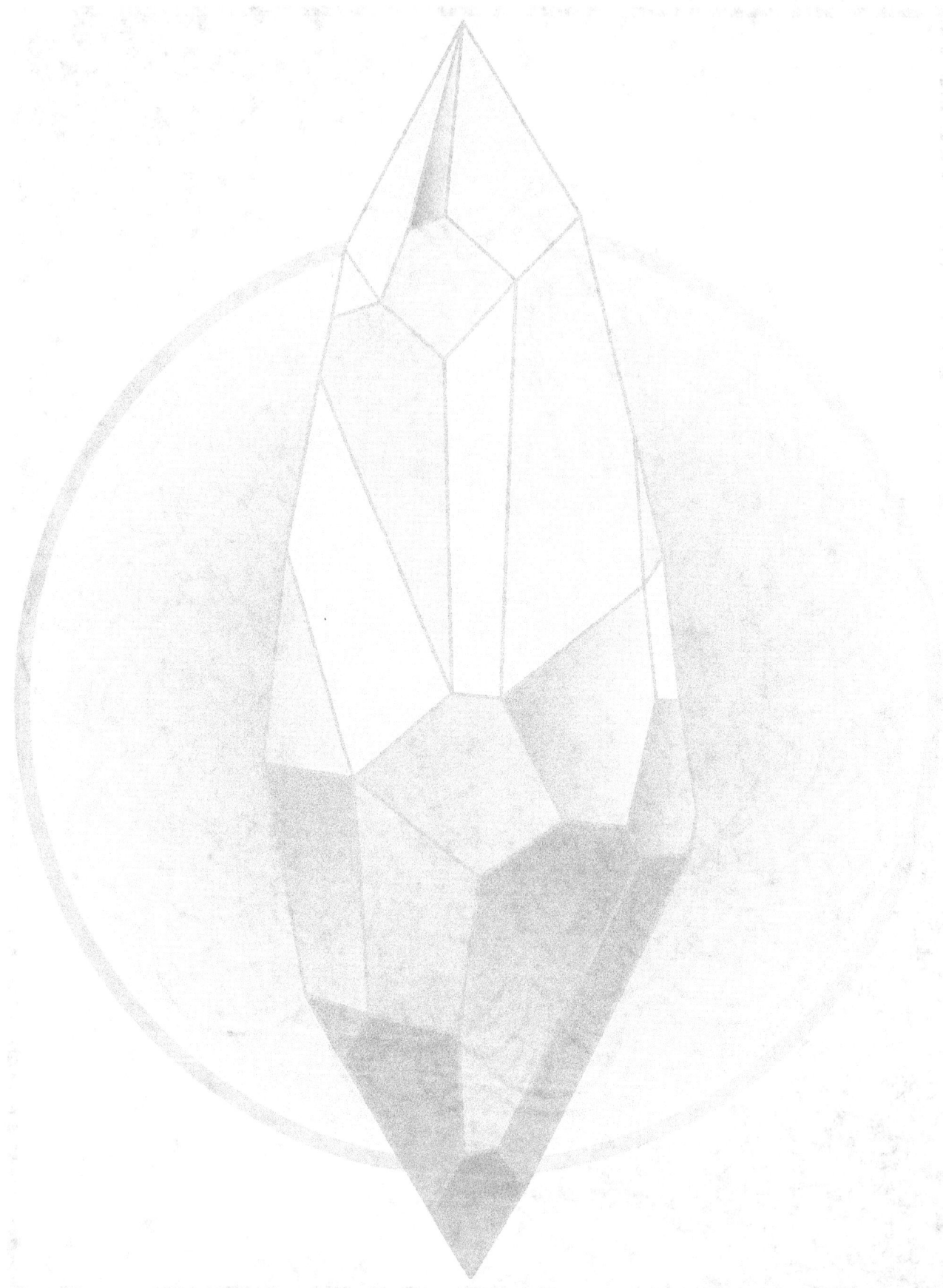

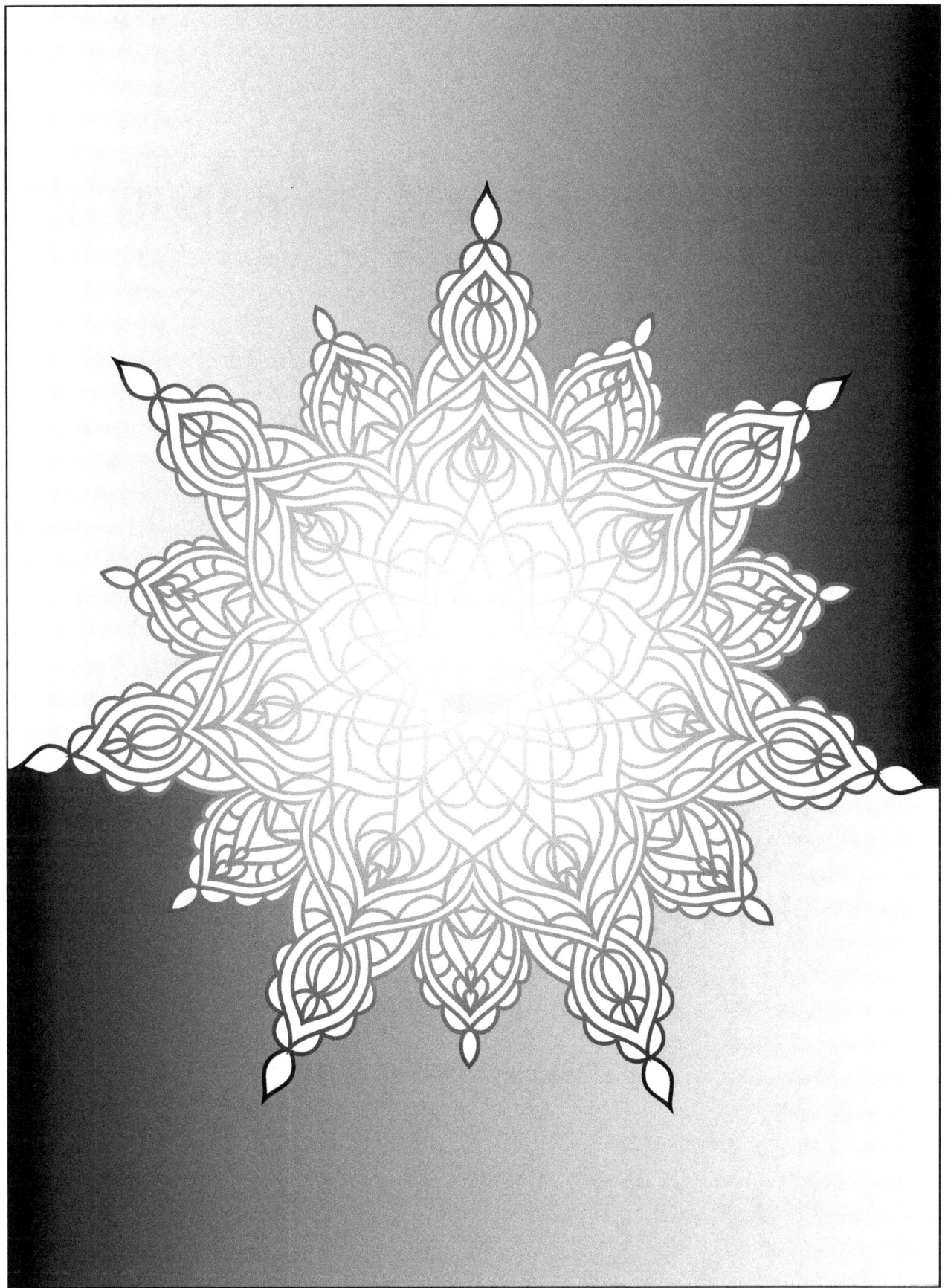

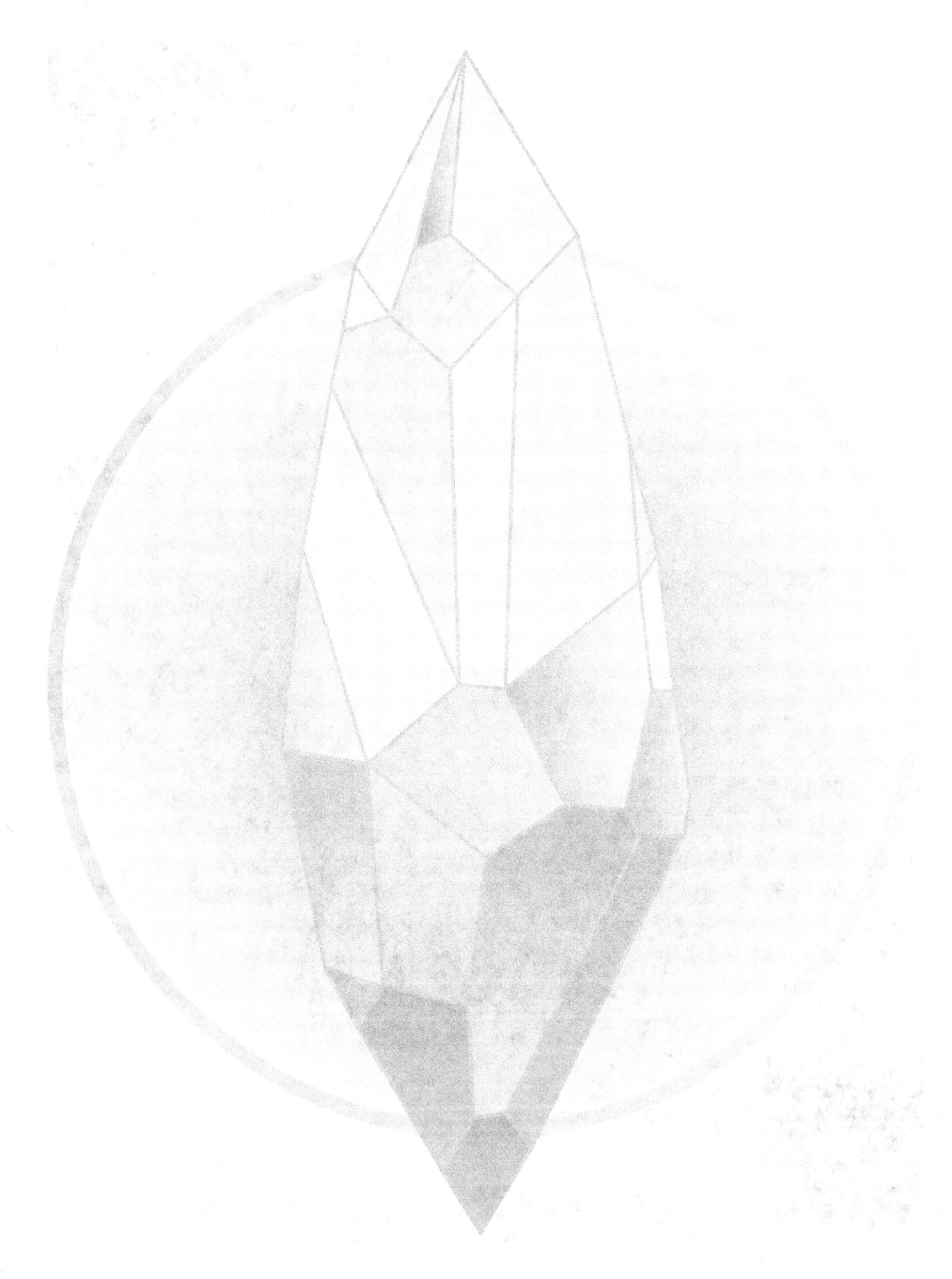

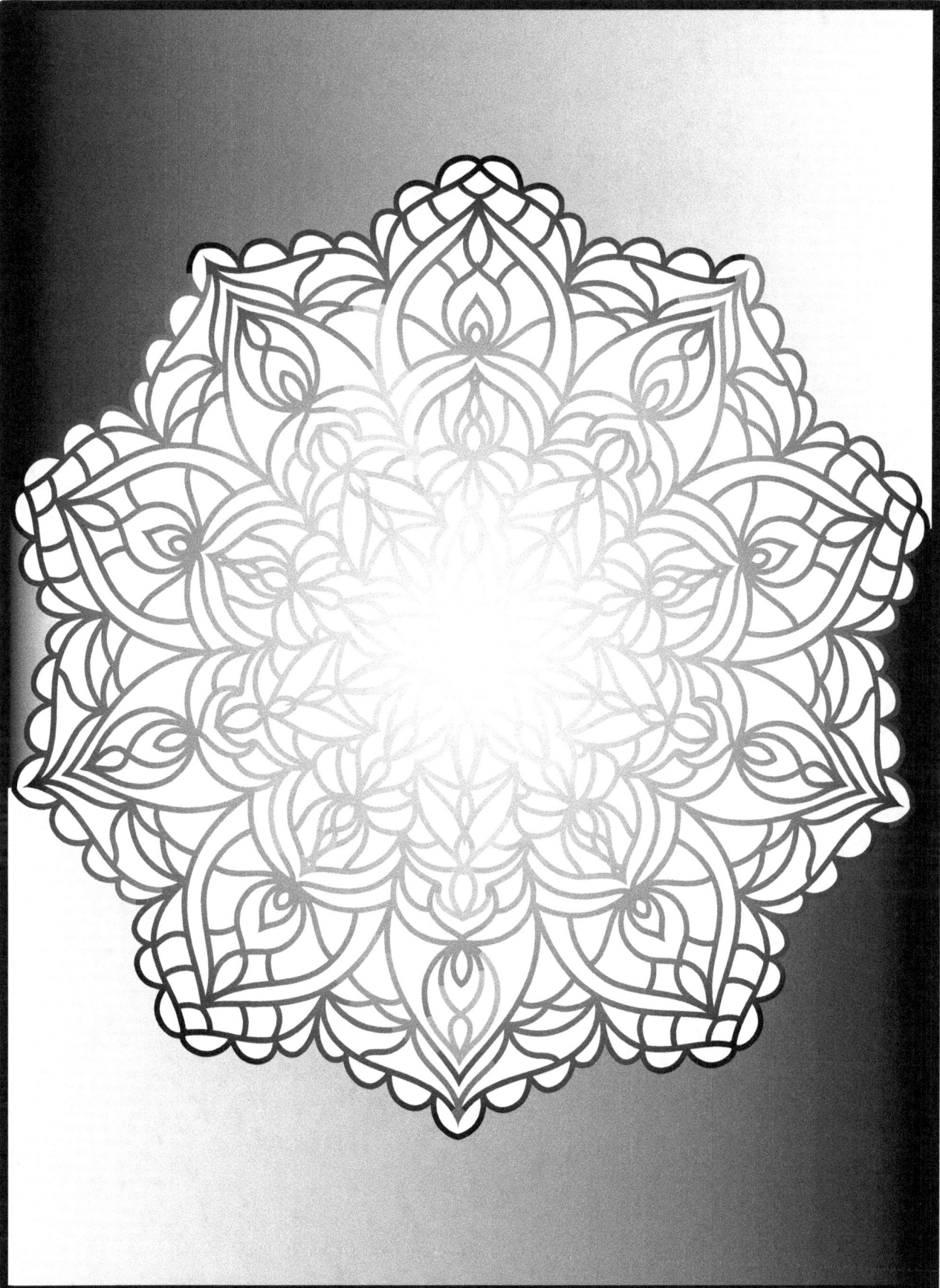

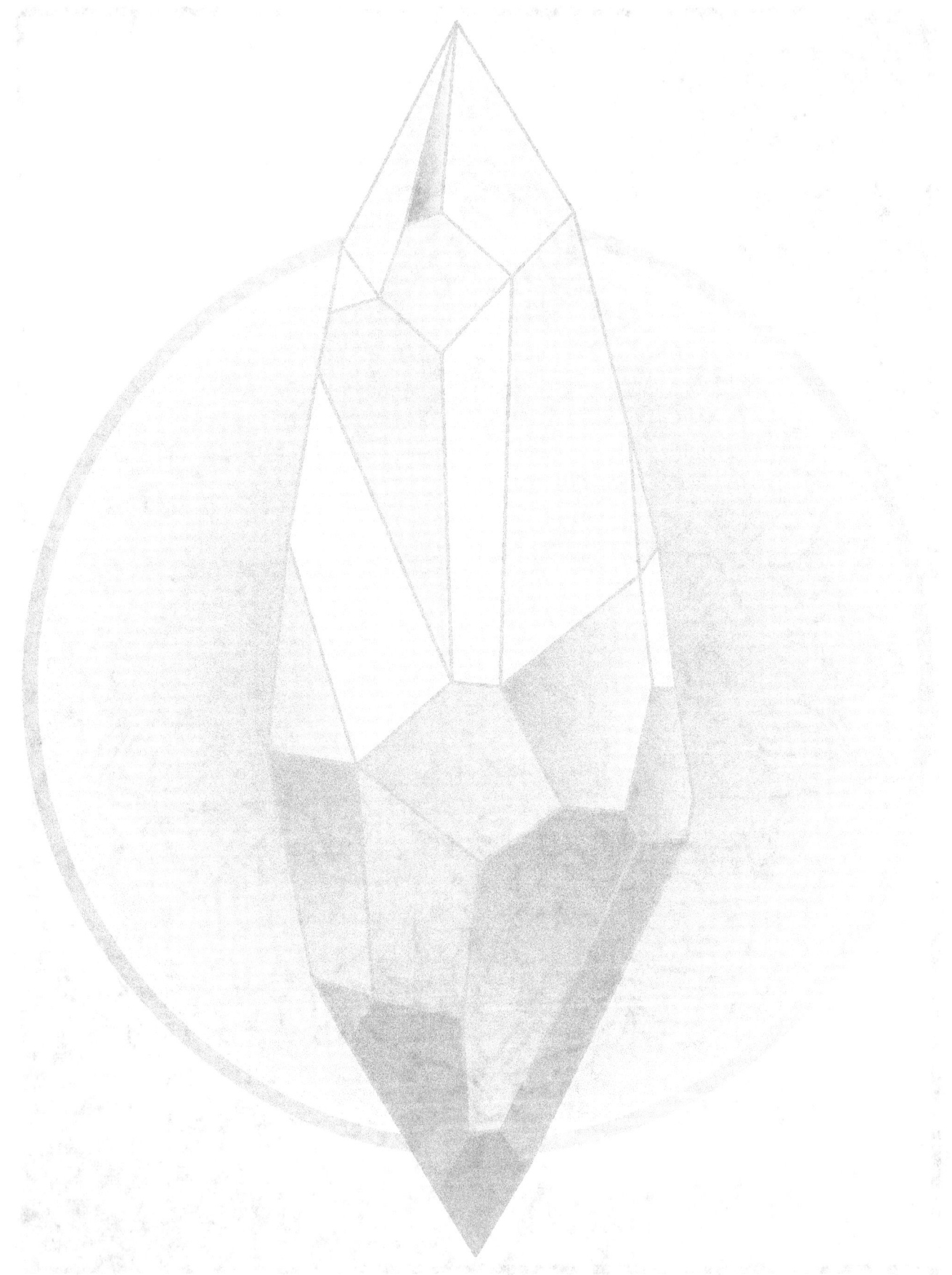

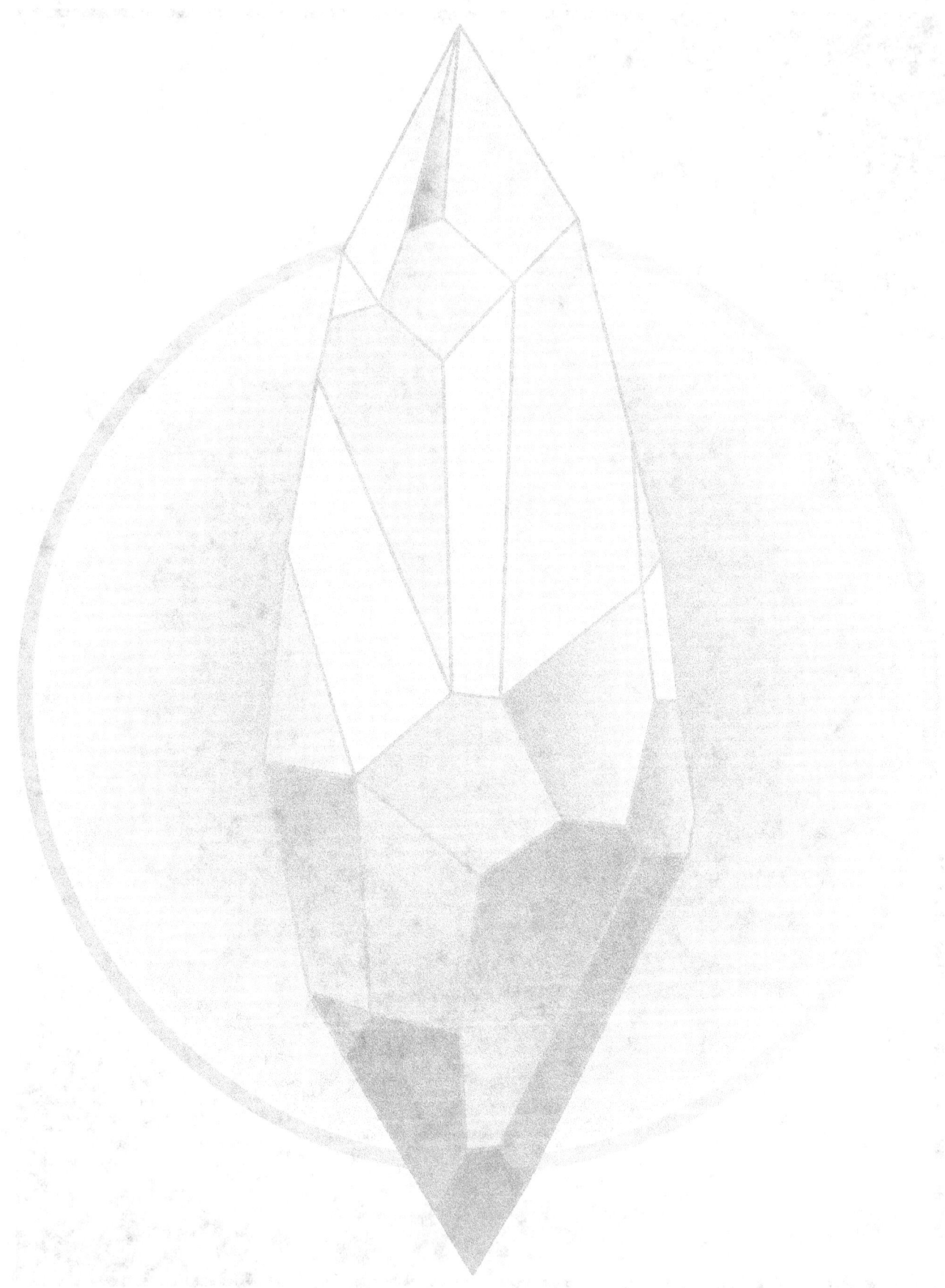

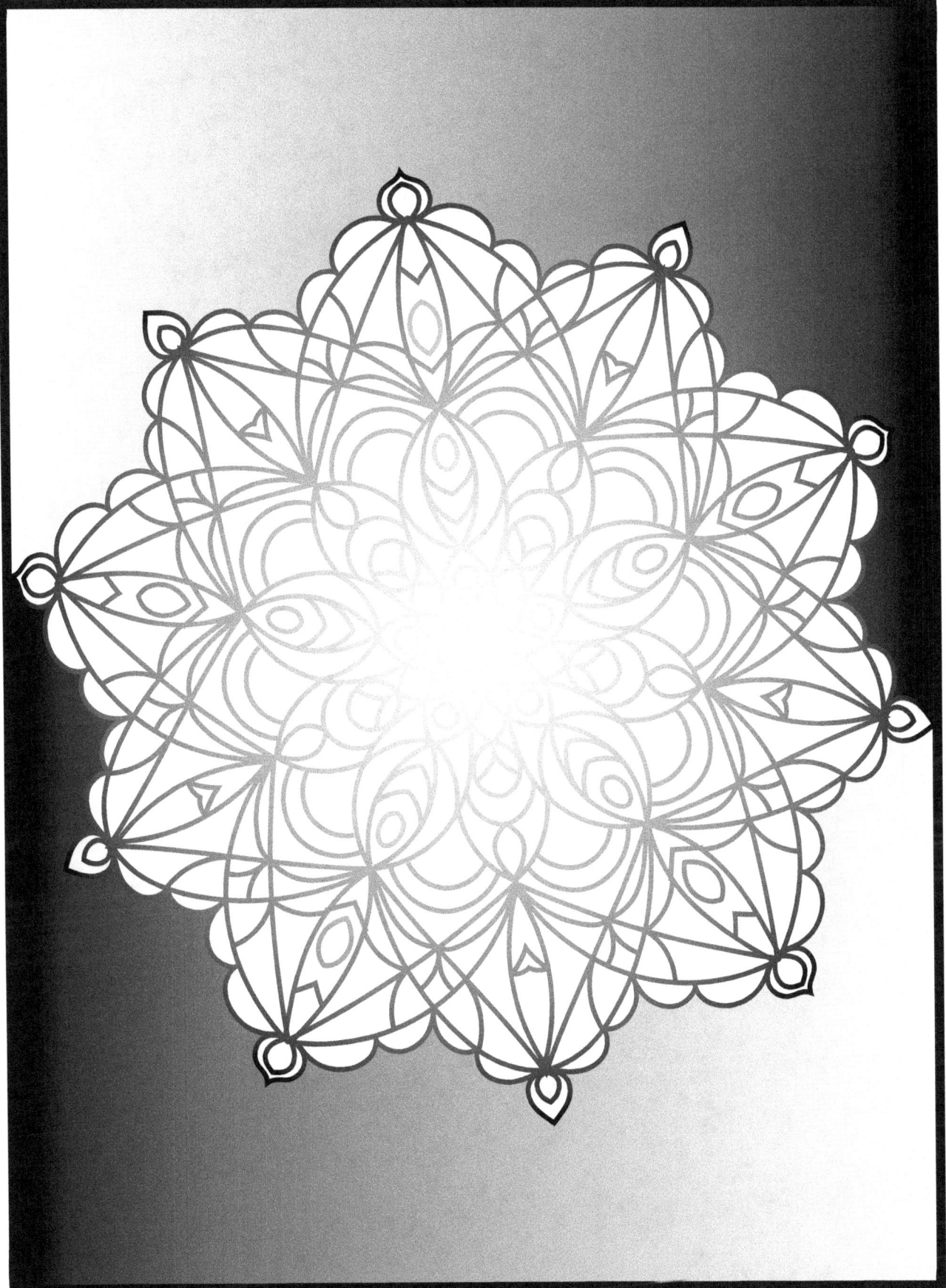

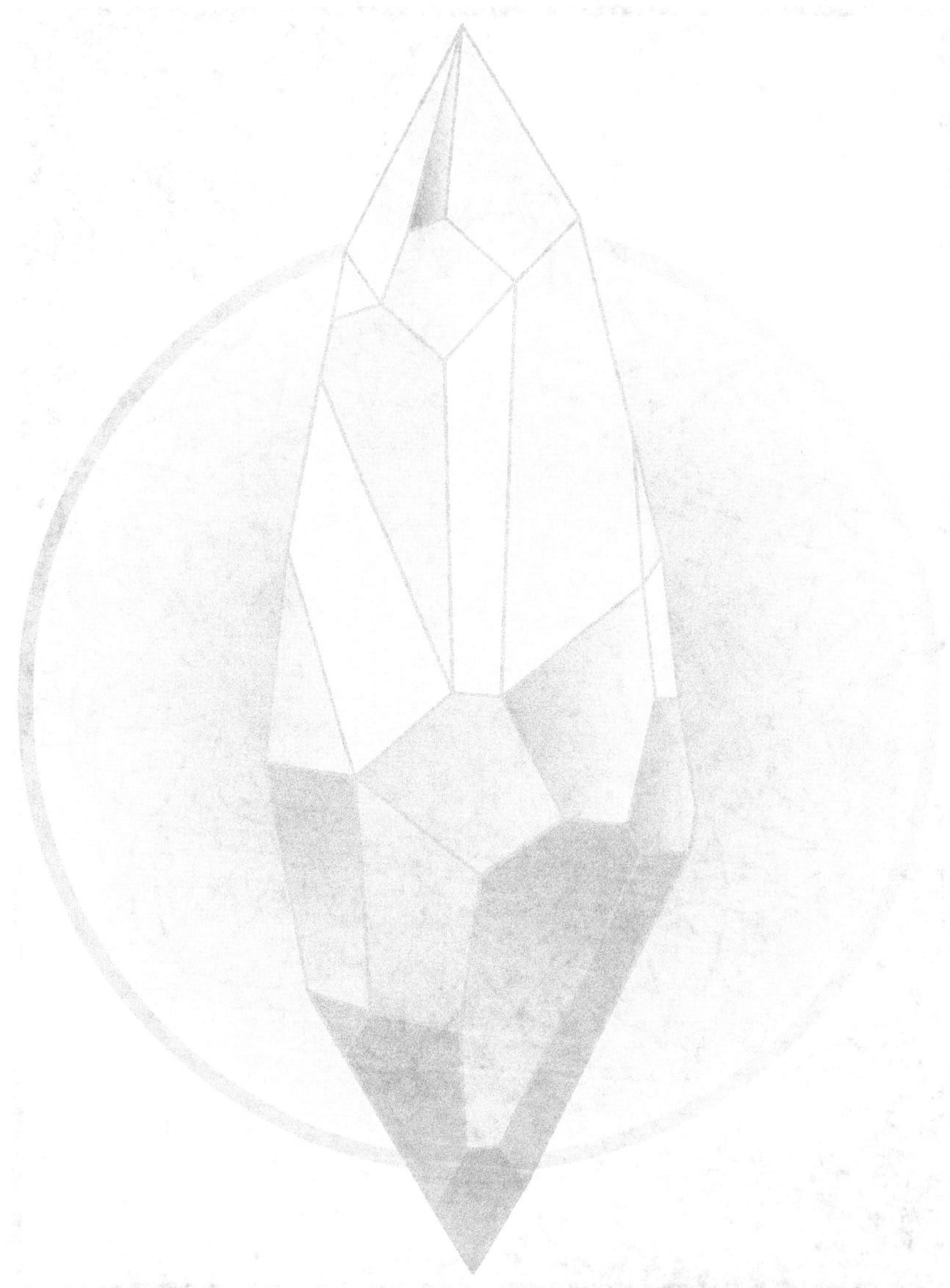

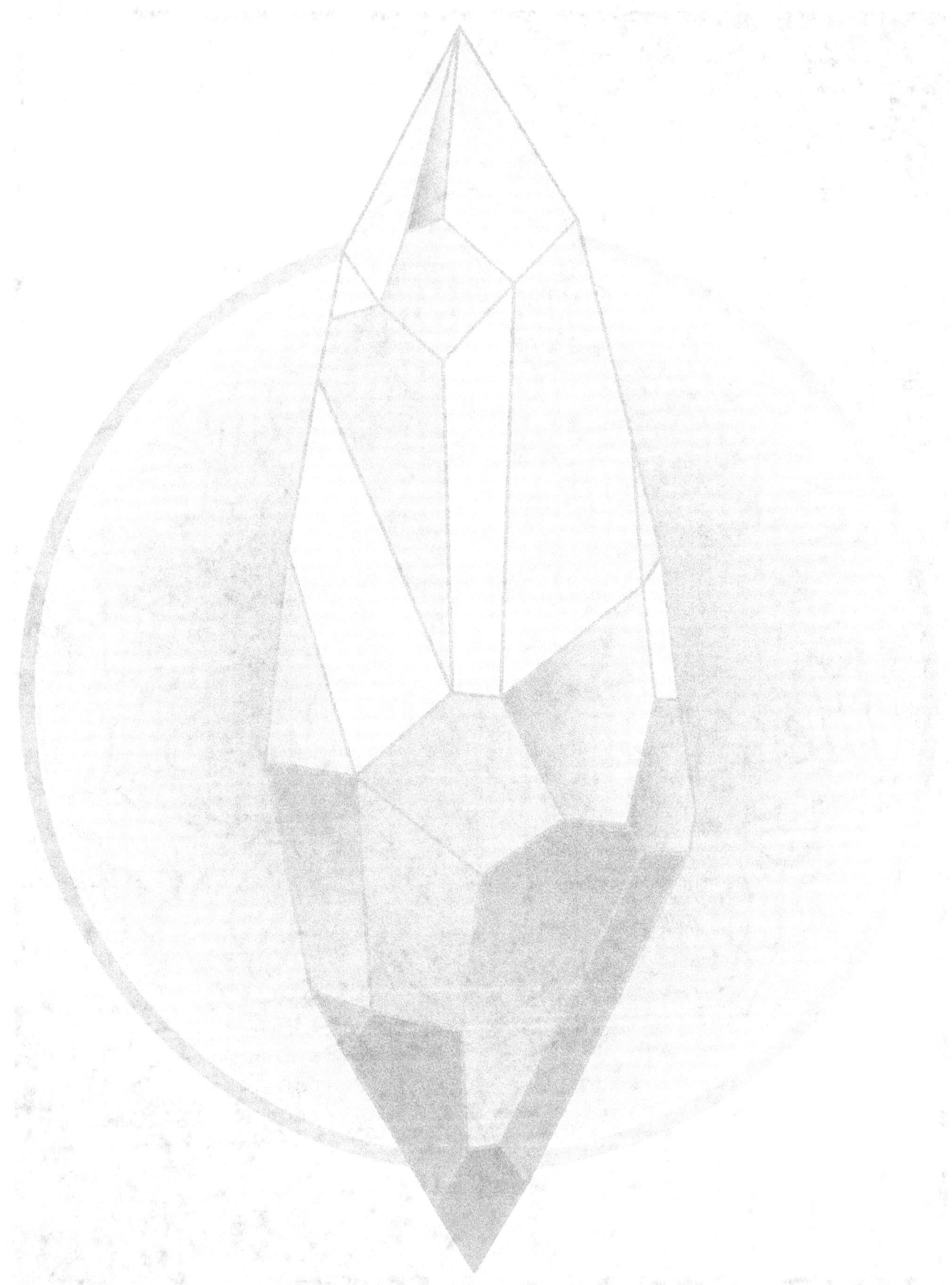

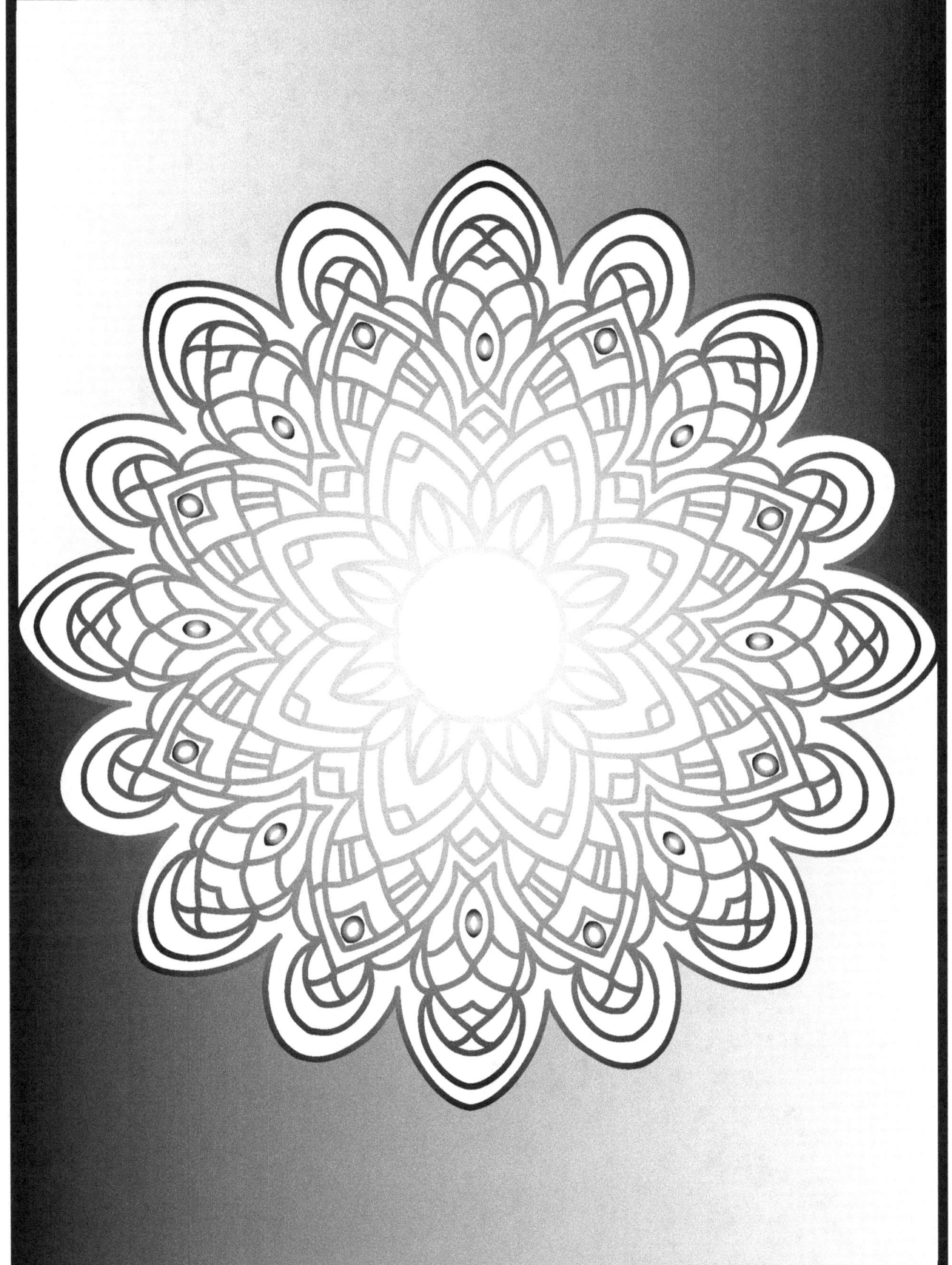

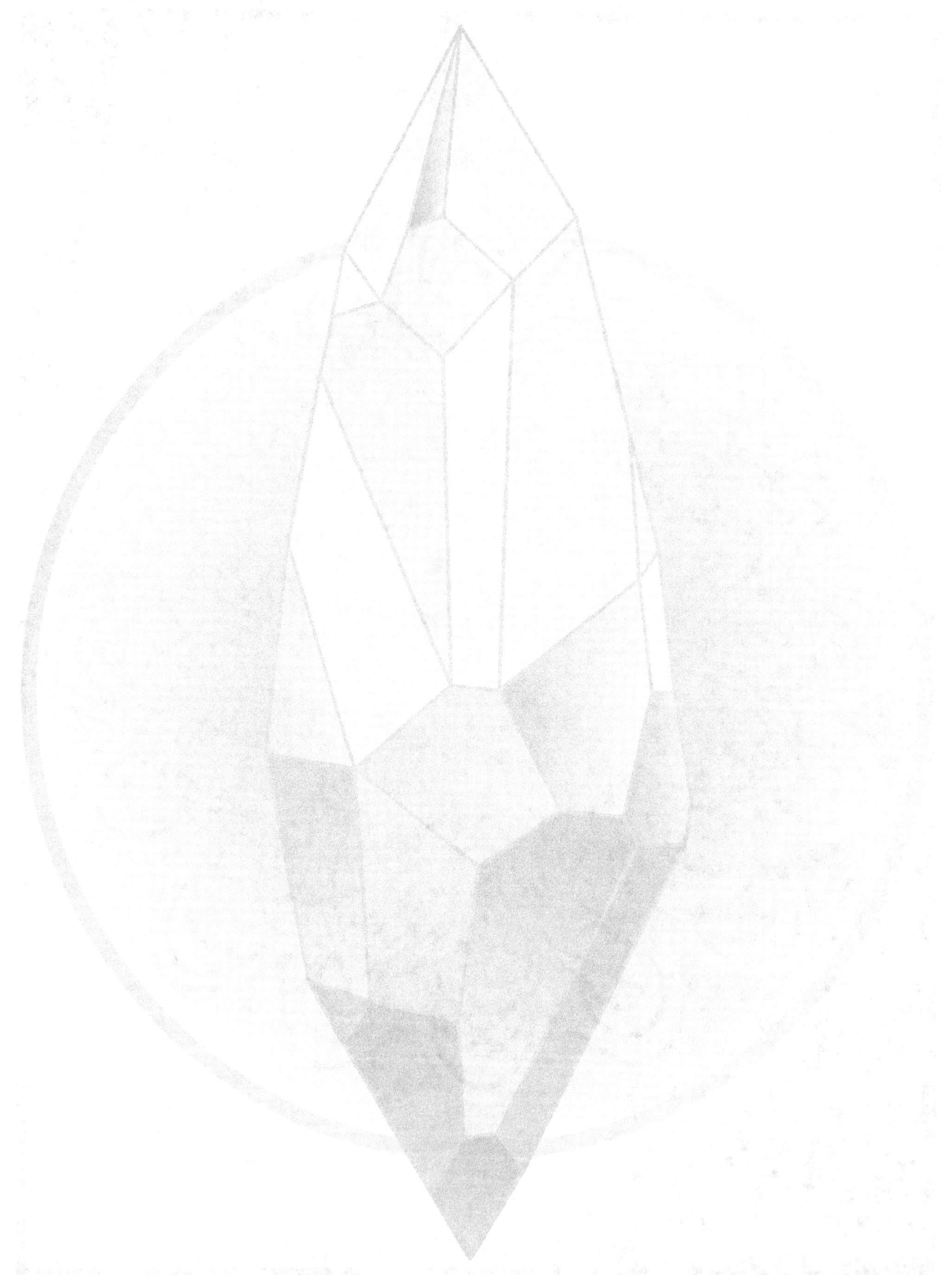

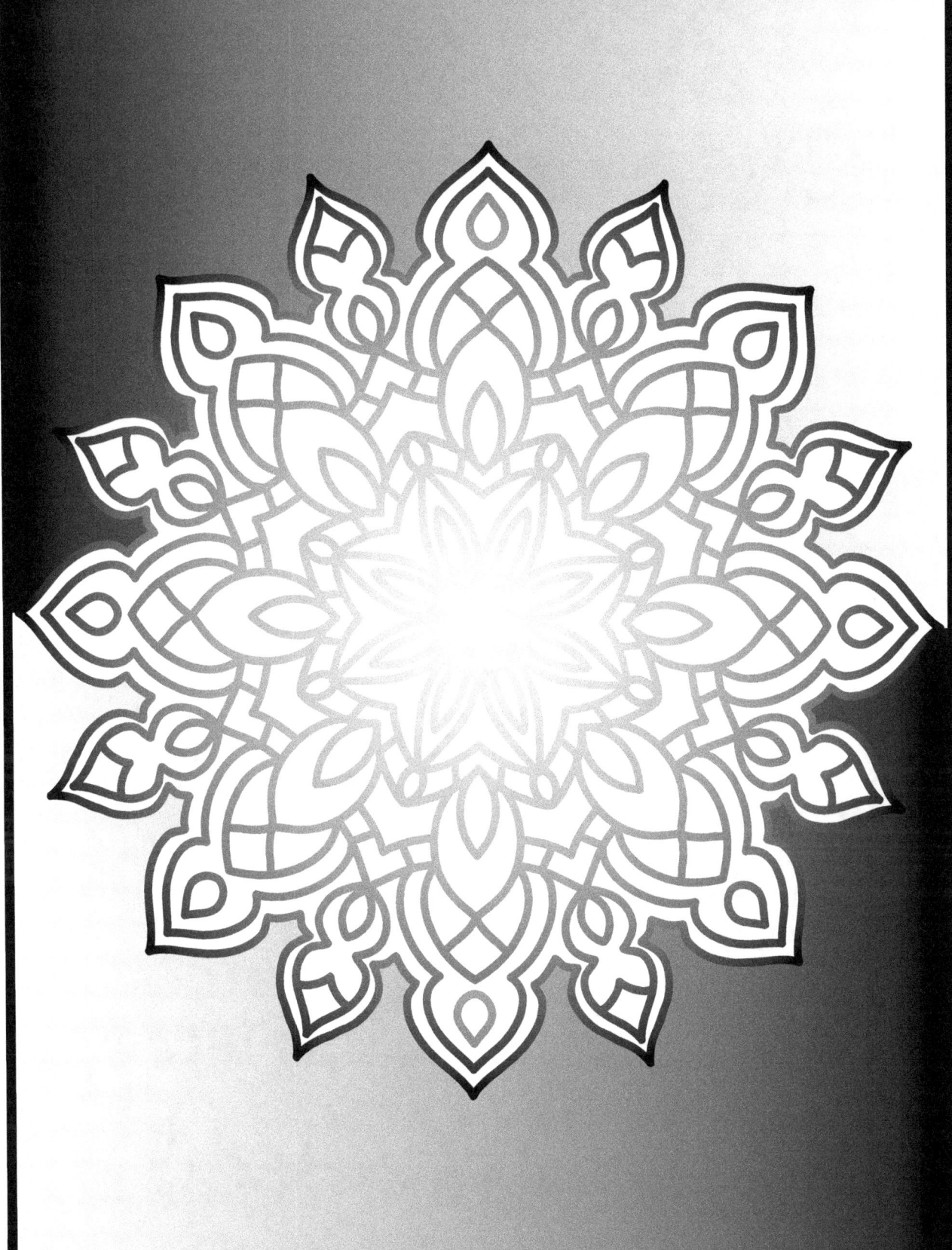

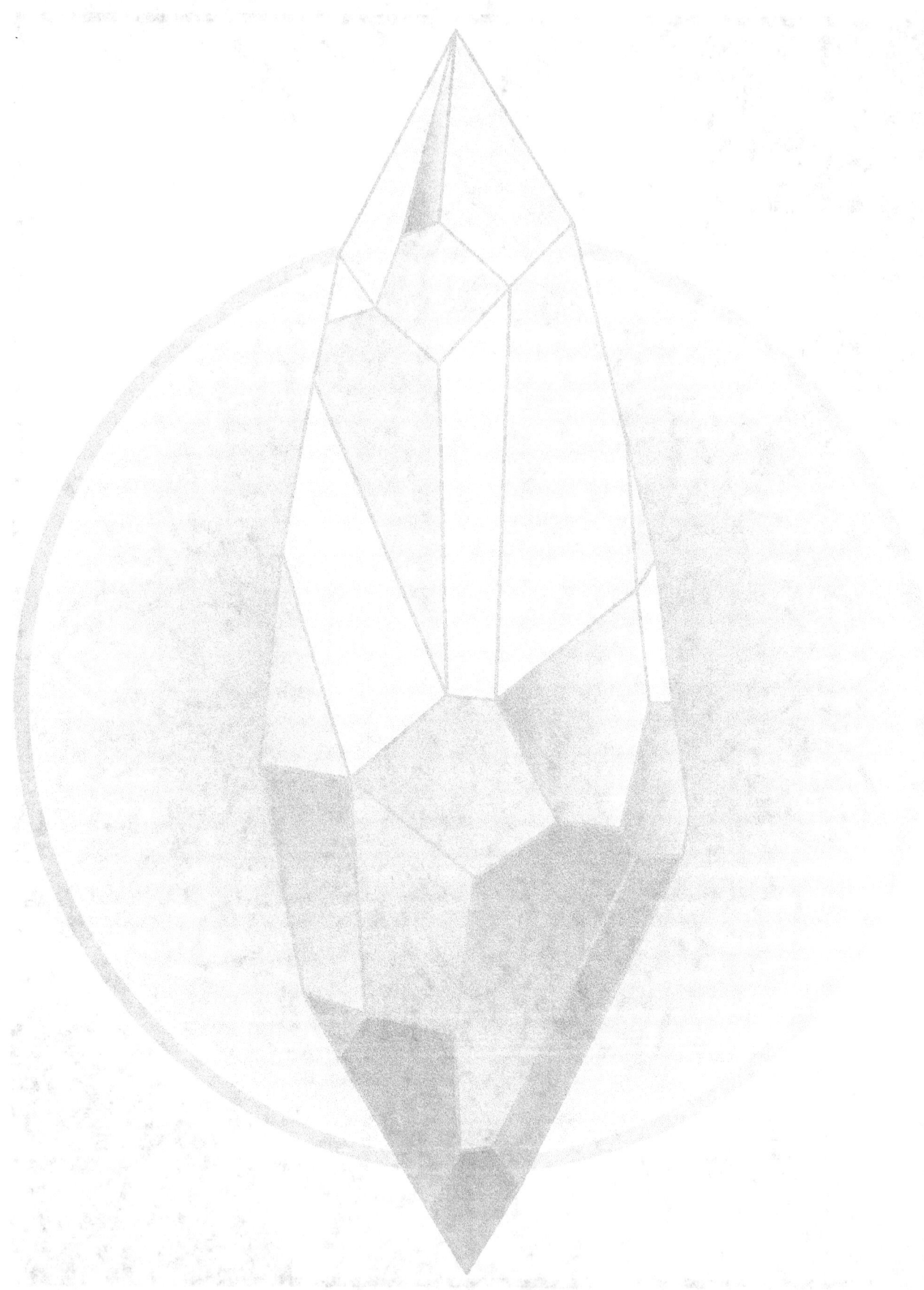

COLOR TEST PAGE

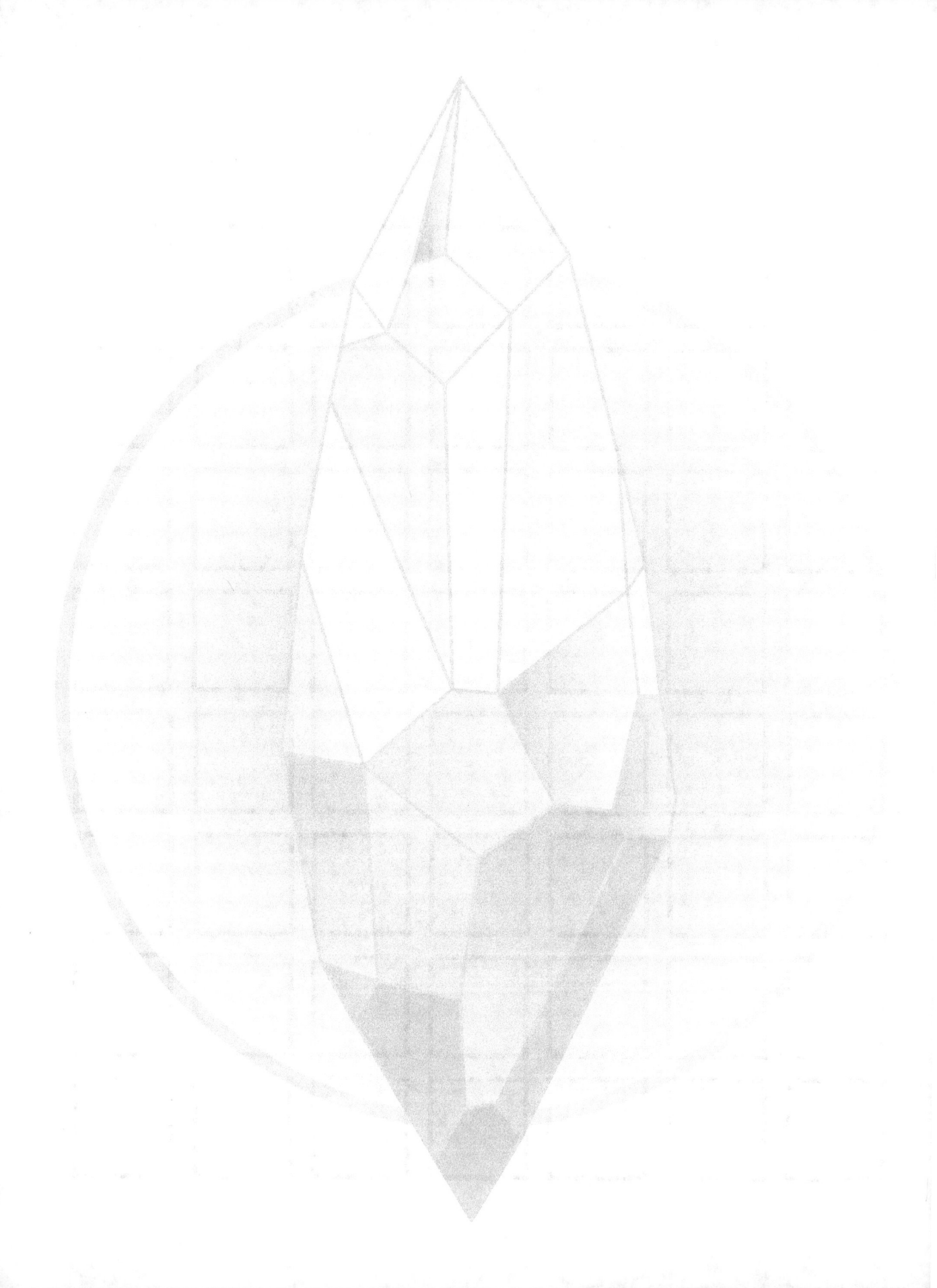

COLOR TEST PAGE

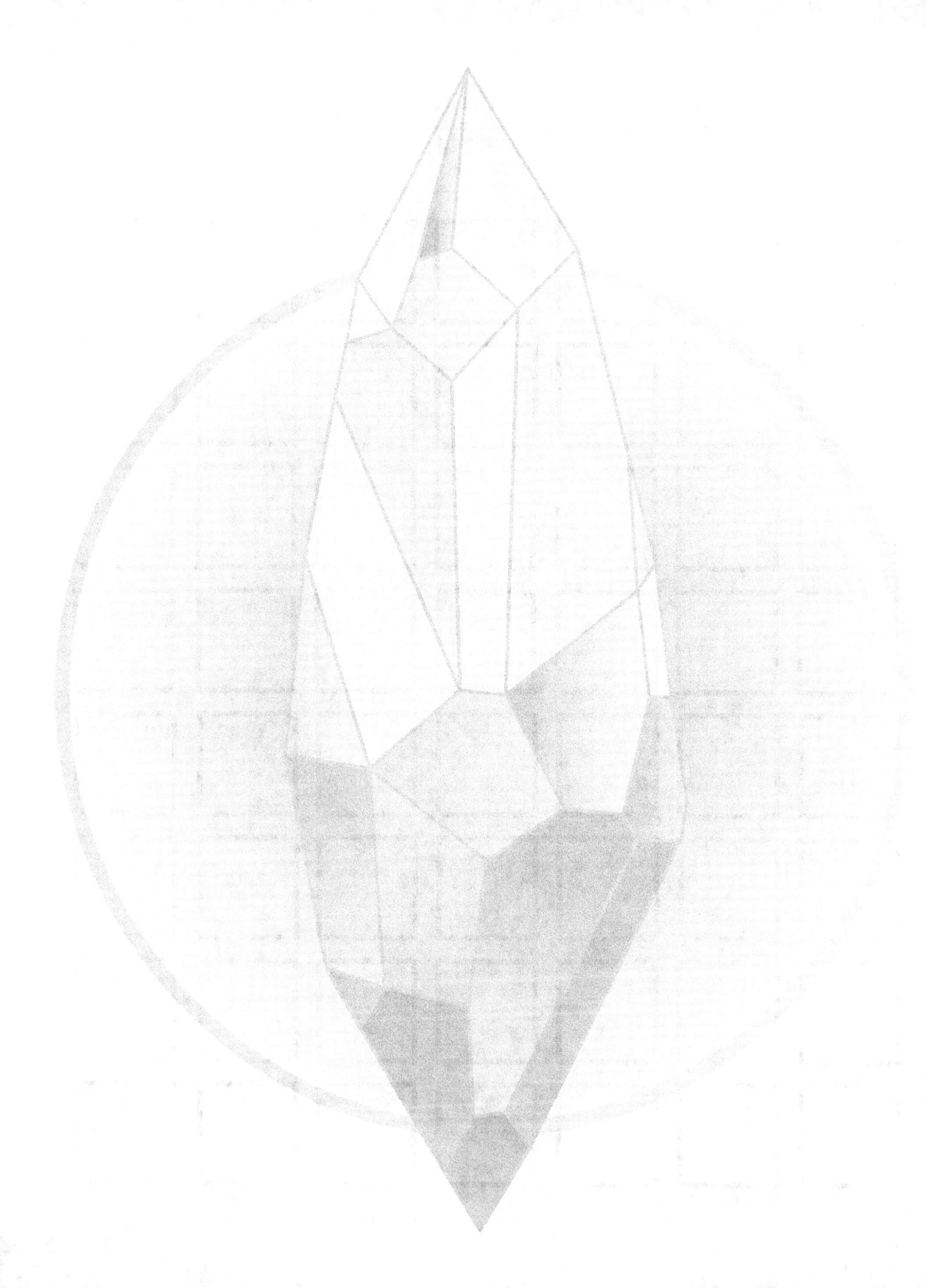

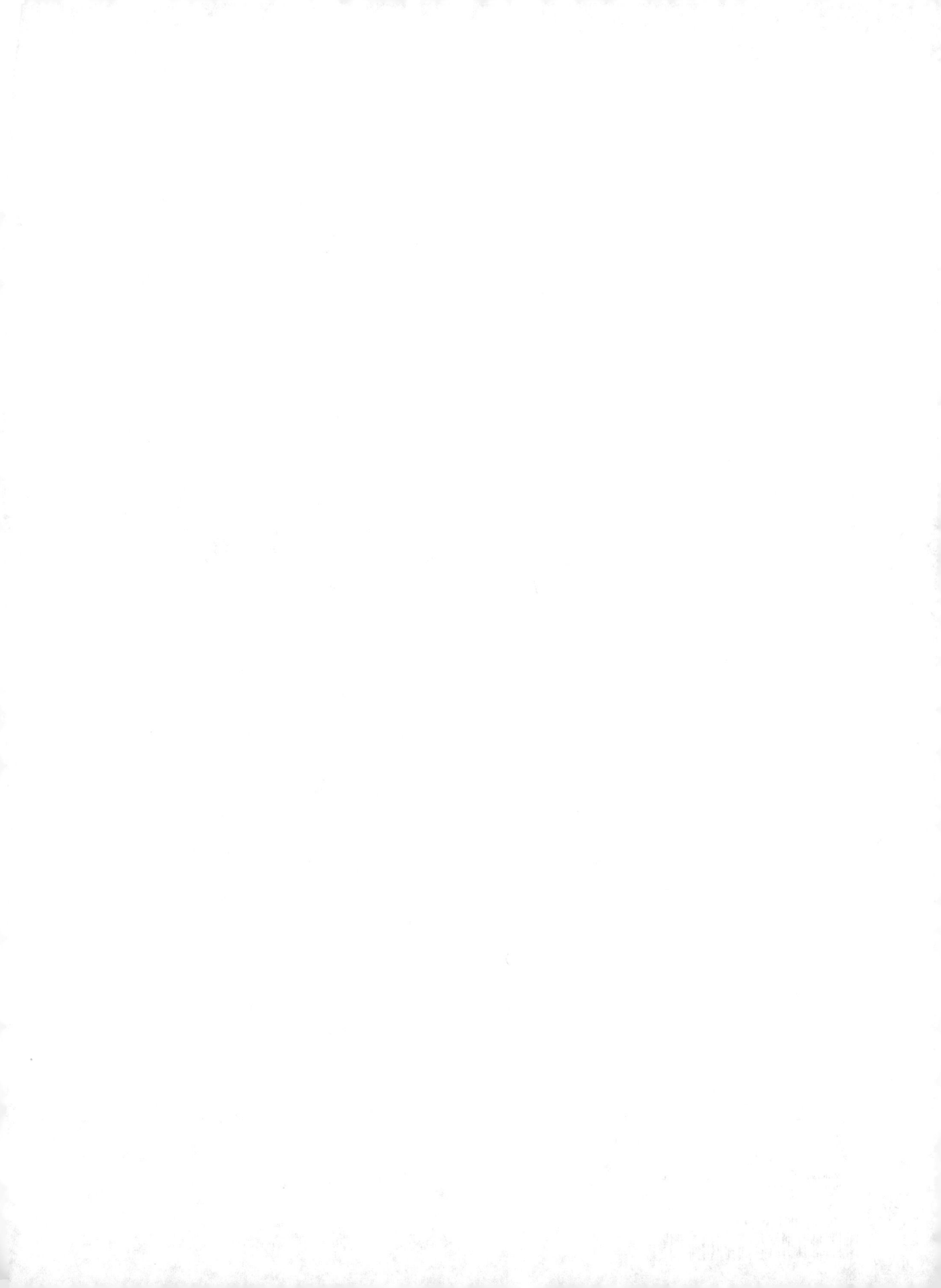

www.ingramcontent.com/pod-product-compliance
Lightning Source LLC
Chambersburg PA
CBHW080620220526
45466CB00010B/3408